SEX AND

CW00486980

An ever
one-act plays for the theatre

by

Diana Amsterdam

SAMUEL FRENCH, INC.
45 WEST 25TH STREET   NEW YORK 10010
7623 SUNSET BOULEVARD HOLLYWOOD 90046
LONDON   TORONTO

Copyright © 1990 by Diana Amsterdam

ALL RIGHTS RESERVED

CAUTION: Professionals and amateurs are hereby warned that the plays collectively published under the title of SEX AND DEATH are subject to royalties. They are fully protected under the copyright laws of the United States of America, the British Commonwealth, including Canada, and all other countries of the Copyright Union. All rights, including professional, amateur, motion pictures, recitation, lecturing, public reading, radio broadcasting, television, and the rights of translation into foreign languages are strictly reserved. In their present form the plays are dedicated to the reading public only.

      The amateur live stage performance rights to the plays collectively published under the title SEX AND DEATH are controlled exclusively by Samuel French, Inc., and royalty arrangements and licenses must be secured well in advance of presentation. PLEASE NOTE that amateur royalty fees are set upon application in accordance with your producing circumstances. When applying for a royalty quotation and license please give us the number of performances intended, dates of production, your seating capacity and admission fee. Royalties are payable one week before the opening performance of the play to Samuel French, Inc., at 45 West 25th Street, New York, NY 10010-2751; or at 7623 Sunset Blvd., Hollywood, CA 90046-2795, or to Samuel French (Canada), Ltd., 100 Lombard Street, Toronto, Ontario, Canada M5C 1M3.

      Royalty of the required amount must be paid whether the plays are presented for charity or gain and whether or not admission is charged.

      Stock royalty quoted on application to Samuel French, Inc.

      For all other rights than those stipulated above, apply to Susan Schulam Literary Agency, Inc. 454 West 44 th Street, New York, NY 10036.

      Particular emphasis is laid on the question of amateur or professional readings, permission and terms for which must be secured in writing from Samuel French, Inc.

      Copying from this book in whole or in part is strictly forbidden by law, and the right of performance is not transferable.

      Whenever the play is produced the following notice must appear on all programs, printing and advertising for the play: "Produced by special arrangement with Samuel French, Inc."

      Due authorship credit must be given on all programs, printing and advertising for the play.

ISBN 0 573 69199 1   Printed in U.S.A.

No one shall commit or authorize any act or omission by which the copyright of, or the right to copyright, these plays may be impaired.

No one shall make any changes in these plays for the purpose of production.

Publication of these plays does not imply availability for performance. Both amateurs and professionals considering a production are *strongly* advised in their own interests to apply to Samuel French, Inc., for written permission before starting rehearsals, advertising, or booking a theatre.

No part of this book may be reproduced, stored in a retrieval system, or transmitted in any form, by any means, now known or yet to be invented, including mechanical, electronic, photocopying, recording, videotaping, or otherwise, without the prior written permission of the publisher.

IMPORTANT BILLING AND CREDIT REQUIREMENTS

All producers of SEX AND DEATH *must* give credit to the Author of the Play in all programs distributed in connection with performances of the Play and in all instances in which the title of the Play appears for purposes of advertising, publicizing or otherwise exploiting the Play and/or a production. The name of the Author *must* also appear on a separate line, on which no other name appears, immediately following the title, and *must* appear in size of type not less than fifty percent the size of the title type.

SEX AND DEATH

Column A:	Column B:
The Sex Portion of the Evening	The Death Portion of the Evening
One Naked Woman and a Fully-Clothed Man	*The End of I*
Lingerie	
Milk	

NOTE: Theatres may choose to produce only one play, or an entire evening of theatre. To compose an entire evening of theatre, theatres are advised to choose two plays from Column A as well as *The End of I*. (Column B).

The "sex" portion of the evening.

*One Naked Woman
and
a Fully-Clothed Man*

A one-act comedy

One Naked Woman and a Fully Clothed Man was first produced at STUDIO X, Ashland, Oregon, on July 22, 1989. The production was directed and designed by Scott Avery, Artistic Director of STUDIO X.

JANET .... Kim Alyce Ataide
ROBERT .... Bradford J. Whitmore
MOVIEGOERS .... Jack Newalu, Dawn E. Davis
and Margaret Avery

CHARACTERS

JANET (mid-thirties)
ROBERT (mid-thirties)

TIME: The present

SETTING: A movie theatre

ONE NAKED WOMAN AND A FULLY-CLOTHED MAN

A movie theatre.

*ROBERT and JANET, in flickering MOVIELIGHT, are
    seated side-by-side in the fully packed theatre. THEY
    hold hands and gaze at the screen.*

*ROBERT holds a container of popcorn between his legs.
    THEY are both munching.*

*Several aspects of the play are left to the discretion of the
    director. JANET's MONOLOGUE, her ongoing
    thoughts, can be either spoken or done with a Voice
    Over. Similarly, THE MOVIEGOERS can be real
    bodies on stage, or merely suggested by shadow and
    lighting.*

JANET'S MONOLOGUE. I look a lot like her. (*Beat.*)
My hair is a lot like her hair. I wonder if Robert notices.
My hair looks a lot like that when the light shines through
it. (*Beat.*) Robert and I are going to go to the mountains
some day. We'll sit near a lake just like that one. Isn't it
pretty? So pristine. Breathtaking. I am going to see
something breathtaking like that some day. (*Beat.*) I could
be that woman. Robert doesn't look like that man, though.
Robert is really a thousand times better-looking than that
man. Aren't I lucky? They're having a good time together.
I wonder if they're falling in love. Of course they are. In
the movies they always fall in love. (*Sighs. Eats popcorn.
Watches, content.*) Robert and I are already in love. (*Beat.*)
I'm so glad we came to see this romantic movie and not
that violent suspense film he wanted to watch at home.
Robert doesn't understand that I can't really relax at home.
I'm always listening for the children and I'm always
worrying about the dishes, the dustballs, the—look how he

9

kisses her. Robert kisses me like that. Robert used to kiss me like that on the dock at Lake Mohegan—

(*JANET watches, munches, content. ROBERT finds a bad kernel of popcorn and throws it on the floor.*)

JANET'S MONOLOGUE. Hahah! I don't have to pick that up! I don't have to worry about the floor! I don't have to give a damn about the floor here! (*Takes a handful of popcorn, throws it on the floor, stomps on it.*)
THE MOVIEGOERS. (*Heard as a chorus of VOICES coming from all around.*) Shhh!

(*JANET giggles. ROBERT pats her hand.*)

JANET'S MONOLOGUE. He probably doesn't have the foggiest idea why I did that. Of course he doesn't. Robert has the most amazing capacity to escape, even at home. Jason can be using his leg as a ramp in a parking garage and Robert just sits there, reading the newspaper. And I get angry at him! I do! If we were home right now, I'd be angry at him just for enjoying himself! Just for escaping into his own private haven while I'm left with the dishes and the dustballs—that woman on the screen wouldn't get angry at him. She'd be happy for her man. Happy ever after. Of course, that man is not the sort who leaves his coffee cups around, who drops his towels right on the floor half the time— (*SHE is getting annoyed. But the movie captures her attention.*) I am that woman on the screen. I am going to go away soon. And have numerous big adventures. I'm going to stay in a hotel just like that one, and wear a silk blouse just like that one. I'm still young. I'm still attractive. Look how he looks at her. Nobody knows how to look at a woman better than my Robert knows how to look at a woman.

(*JANET turns to look at ROBERT, and stares at him so
hard that HE looks at her, smiles, pats her hand, turns
back to the screen. SHE turns back to the screen.*)

JANET'S MONOLOGUE. Omigod! When did that
happen? Why do they do this to people? There's probably
one woman in this entire theatre who looks like that and
that one woman is sitting up tall and proud while the rest
of us are shrinking. You gotta admit they're beautiful,
though. Beautiful breasts are beautiful. The female form is
beautiful. I have a female form. Robert. Don't look. It's
just that my female form has had three children, my breasts
have nursed three fat babies, my breasts have served as
pacifiers and teething rings—My breasts are real breasts—
Real. Saggy. Ruined. Don't look! He's looking. I wonder
if he's noticing. Comparing her breasts to mine— (*SHE
grabs a handful of popcorn, stuffs it in her mouth, several
kernels fall onto her bosom. SHE gives a little shriek.*)

THE MOVIEGOERS. Shhh!

(*JANET rummages in her dress for the various kernels of
popcorn. ROBERT glances at her.*)

JANET. (*In actual dialogue, to Robert. Whispers as
SHE rummages in her dress.*) Darling, remind me to find
Jason's galoshes when we get home.

(*JANET and ROBERT turn back to the movie.*)

JANET'S MONOLOGUE. How much footage can you
take of one woman's breasts? So when she throws up her
arms they bobble up and down, big deal, toss up a cabbage
that comes down, too, why don't they show us five

minutes of cole slaw? Slow motion. Only a male director
would do this. Only a male director would ever assume that
an entire audience would be interested in fifteen minutes of
footage of one woman's breasts. (*SHE glances around the
theatre.*) And he's right. The entire audience is glued to that
screen. Every last eye in the place, glued. When he was
showing footage of the majestic Alps, everyone was
fidgeting but plaster a coupla boobies up there and people
stop breathing. I can understand it with the men. But you'd
think the women would rebel. You'd think the women
would turn and talk to one another, show snapshots of our
children, or get up on the seats and dance, *something*. I'd
like to see 500 men sit like house plants for 25 minutes
while some female director exhibits the bobbling capacity
of the male penis in slow motion. Sure. I'm afraid to look
at him. His lips are probably parted. There's probably a
thin stream of drool oozing from his mouth.

(*JANET reaches over to touch Robert's lips. HE kisses her
    fingertips.*)

JANET'S MONOLOGUE. I'm such a fool. He's not
thinking about that woman's breasts at all, he's thinking
about me, he's thinking about how beautiful it is to be
sitting next to a woman whose breasts have been used for
the furtherance of life, who has really made something of
her breasts.

(*ROBERT kisses the empty air.*)

JANET'S MONOLOGUE. Reflex.

(*JANET and ROBERT sit and watch the movie. ROBERT
    has stopped eating popcorn.*)

JANET. Popcorn, dear?

(*JANET takes a handful of popcorn and holds it directly before his eyes. HE takes a kernel and eats it, then pulls her hand down and pats it.*)

JANET'S MONOLOGUE. Oh, no. What now? Is it going to be? Is it going to be that kind of movie? Lillian. Why didn't you tell me it was going to be that kind of movie? Lillian. You're supposed to be my best friend. Okay. Switch. Switch. Switch now. Enough. Enough. We get the message. Plot line extended. I can't move. I hope he doesn't notice me here. These Italian movies. These Italian directors. Mr. Capistrani or whatever your name is, did it ever occur to you to that not everybody wants to watch this on a Wednesday night? Some people have jobs. Some people have families. Sure. The men like it. What man wouldn't like, what man and he's not even that good-looking wouldn't like a beautiful woman to do that to him with her bare breasts? But did it ever occur to you, Mr. Cappelini, that most of these men are here with their wives? Their wives? Robert doesn't fall for this. Robert won't allow himself to be a pawn in some Italian director's wet dream.

(*ROBERT is watching the movie.*)

JANET'S MONOLOGUE. This is ridiculous. He's just watching the movie. They're all just watching the movie. You come to the movies to watch the movie so that's what everybody is doing, watching the movie. (*SHE watches the movie.*)
JANET. (*Inadvertently.*) Ladeda!
THE MOVIEGOERS. Shhh!

JANET'S MONOLOGUE. Switch. Switch. He's taking off her high heels. He's lifting her skirt. He's pulling down her panties. Thank God her skirt is still on. He's taking off his shirt. He's putting her in a chair. He's spilling water on her. Or is it champagne? He's licking it off. Sucking it off. She's opening her mouth. He's drinking the champagne. He's kissing the champagne into her open mouth. My God. I wonder if Robert is thinking about sex. I wonder if he's noticing how clammy our hands are getting? I can't take my hand from his hand. If I take my hand from his hand, it'll make a glopping sound. This is no time for a glopping sound. I can't move. Did it ever occur to you, Mr. Capillary, that not everybody wants to watch this? Some people have jobs. Some people have children. Some people have not made love like that in ten years. (*SHE reaches for the bucket of popcorn, misses, pulls back her hand.*) Omigod! I touched something! Something hard! Tell me it was Robert's thigh! Only why would his thigh be above the popcorn? Robert would never. He would never. Never at a time like this. I've got to get my hand out of his. My hand is clamming all over his. Or maybe his hand is clamming all over mine. Oh, look there. Isn't that sweet? That man is putting his arm around that woman. They're not married. The best thing is to sit still. Withdraw all energy from one's hand and sit still. Sit very, very still. This will all be over soon. (*Several beats.*) Very soon. (*SHE closes her eyes. Opens them.*) Oh, good. They're finally doing it. He's on the chair and she's on his lap and I think I think the director intends us to think that they are actually having sex now. She's completely naked on his lap with that beautiful hair which I now see is nothing like mine streaming down her back soaked with sweat or is it champagne or water and she is writhing around on him and he is fully dressed, nice touch, Mr. Pastrami or whatever the hell your name is, nice touch his hands on her ass like that, squeezing her ass with those immaculate white shirt-sleeves those expensive silver cuff links, very ironic. My hand is a stinking cesspool. I have to get it away—

JANET. (*Yells aloud, points to ceiling.*) Look there!

(*ROBERT looks, SHE extricates her hand from his, wipes her hand on her blouse and wipes his hand on his shirt and places his hand on his knee and resumes normal pose.*)

THE MOVIEGOERS. Shhh!

JANET'S MONOLOGUE. I don't believe he noticed. He's turned into a zombie. My Robert's turned into a zombie. Are you satisfied now, Mr. Bologne? Forcing us all into an act of voyeurism? Is this your idea of power? Reminding us of things we mean to forget—

(*ROBERT, without taking his eyes from the screen, removes the container of popcorn from between his legs, places it on the floor, and crosses his legs.*)

JANET'S MONOLOGUE. Omigod. My marriage is over. My husband has gotten a massive erection watching some Italian director's movie of a naked woman sitting on the lap of a fully-clothed man. Robert! Darling! I'll take off my clothes! I'll sit on your lap! I'll writhe! I'll arch my back! I'll grow my hair! I'll lose fifteen pounds! Everything! Everything! We'll bring back the magic, Robert, we will! Tonight! Tonight I'll be just like that woman on the screen! Just like! Better! Better!

(*ROBERT uncrosses his legs.*)

JANET'S MONOLOGUE. Or maybe—he doesn't have an erection. I must know. And it's so goddamn dark in here. (*Very slowly moves toward him, leans down over him, peers more and more closely at his crotch until SHE is almost touching it. The following is in whispers.*)

    ROBERT. What are you doing?

    JANET. Hello, dear.

    ROBERT. Are you sleepy?

    JANET. No, I'm looking for something. I think I saw it. And now it's gone.

    ROBERT. What?

    JANET. Nothing.

    ROBERT. What is it? I'll help you find it.

    JANET. You'll help me find it.

    ROBERT. Of course, if you tell me what it is ... An earring? Your contact lens?

    JANET. (*Stands, shouts.*) Our love! I'm looking for our love! Our passion! What happened to it? We used to be like that! My breasts were never quite that big but in every other way, Robert, we couldn't keep our hands off each other, we looked forward all day to coming home and ripping each other's clothes off, climbing all over each other, attacking each other! And now you sit in this movie theatre and get more excited watching some made-up foreign actress writhe her phony rump around than you do when I walk around our bedroom stark naked and you sit there reading! Reading! Stark naked! Reading! And I miss it! I miss it, Robert! I want it back! Please, bring it back!

    THE MOVIEGOERS. (*A chorus of VOICES.*) Shh! Shut up! Down in front! Quiet! Get her outta here!

    JANET. (*Noticing them all.*) Oh—well—This is part of the show. (*LIGHTS up. To the moviegoers.*) See? The movie's over. This is part of the show! A very big thing in

Italy now, it's called "theatre at the movies," or "teatro i movieo."

(*JANET applauds. THE MOVIEGOERS applaud.*
JANET slowly sits. JANET and ROBERT sit there, jostled by the moviegoers exiting their seats.
The theater is vacated. JANET and ROBERT remain.)

ROBERT. That was unacceptable behavior.

JANET. I know that.

ROBERT. I think I saw Elliot and Vanessa Mansfield in the audience.

JANET. Oh, God.

ROBERT. There is nothing the matter with our sex life.

JANET. I know that.

ROBERT. It's a perfectly normal sex life for people who have been married as long as we have, with all the responsibilities we have.

JANET. I know.

ROBERT. What could have come over you?

JANET. The movie.

ROBERT. It was a perfectly normal Italian movie. You're the one who wanted to see it. I wanted to stay home and watch *The Great Escape*.

JANET. I know. I'm sorry.

ROBERT. Do you really feel that way, Jan? Because if you do, we're in a lot of trouble.

(*Long beat.*)

JANET. No.

ROBERT. Then we better get home. (*Checks his watch.*) We told Marcie we'd be in by twelve. (*HE picks up his coat, starts to leave.*)

JANET. Robert! When we get home!—Remind me to look for Jason's galoshes.

CURTAIN

COSTUMES

Everyday wear suggesting a suburban couple is appropriate.

PROP LIST

<u>Furniture</u>

Two theatre seats, center stage.
Other theatre seats around or behind them, optional.

<u>Other props</u>

Tub of popcorn—brought on by Robert; large soft drink cup—brought on by Janet; wristwatch worn by Robert.

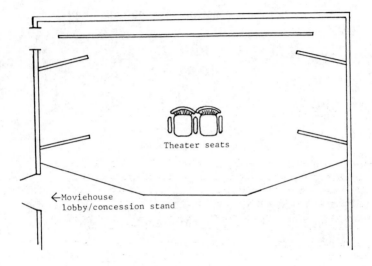
Theater seats
←Moviehouse
lobby/concession stand

''ONE NAKED WOMAN AND A FULLY CLOTHED MAN''

LINGERIE

A one-act comedy

Lingerie was first produced by the Four Riders Theatre Company at the Irish Arts Center, New York, New York, on June 13, 1989.

MAX...David Sterry
SALLY...Patti Sheehan
SABRINA ....Judith Elaine

Director.. Jenifer Goode
Set ....David Katz

CHARACTERS

MAX (mid-thirties)
SALLY (early twenties)
SABRINA (mid-thirties)

TIME: The Present

SETTING: Composite setting representing a park, a living room with telephone, and a bedroom.

LINGERIE

SCENE: New York City. A recent summer.

The action takes place in three settings: a park, a bedroom, and a living room. Very few objects are needed to depict these settings. The park needs only a bench and a moon glowing in the skies. The bedroom need only be a bed or even just the edge of a bed and a mirror. The living room need show only a small table with a telephone, and a chair.

Lighting should be kept on the dark side, with illumination on the characters and their immediate surroundings.

MAXWELL is a charming man in his late thirties. HE has the slightly mussed look of an intellectual; yet his casual, artsy clothing is expensive. In style and look, he's a trend-setter, very attractive.

SALLY is a lovely young woman in her early twenties. SHE is the picture of natural, country beauty: brunette, rosy-cheeked, and wholesome. SHE wears white blouses with little round collars, and full skirts with flowers, and sandals. SHE speaks with an unalloyed southern accent.

SABRINA is a sexy woman in her mid-thirties. Her hair is wild, her eyes are ringed by not unattractive brown shadows, she is visually interesting.

AT RISE: LIGHTS up.

Scene 1
The Park

A radiant full moon hangs in the heavens. MAXWELL and SALLY sit on a park bench, a couple of lovebirds.

MAX. It's never happened to me.

SALLY. Never?

MAX. In fifteen years. But I've seen it.

SALLY. What did you do?

MAX. I ran.

SALLY. You didn't!

MAX. No, no, of course not, I stopped it, I grabbed the guy and held him till the cops came.

SALLY. My goodness! Daddy told me don't you resist, Sally, if one them wants whatever you give it up, girl. He could've had a knife! ... You are so different from what daddy told me to expect.

MAX. I'm not a mugger.

SALLY. I know that, brown eyes, I mean about men, about New York City men.

MAX. What did your daddy say?

SALLY. My daddy told me, Sally, he told me, all over this great nation, there are men who want to conquer women. Most want to conquer their bodies and leave it at that. But there are some, Sally, there are the very few, who aren't satisfied with just their bodies, Sally, no, they want to conquer their souls, too. They are soul collectors and they keep the souls of pretty little girls like you just like pet fireflies in a jar. And all the soul collectors, you know where they go? New York City. New York City's just a regular magnet for soul collectors.

MAX. (*Throws himself to his knees at her feet.*) Your father's right!

SALLY. Why, Maxwell—

MAX. Sally, Sally!

SALLY. Darling, what is it?

MAX. I've been that sort of man, that exact sort of man your father's describing—

SALLY. You? You are the sweetest person I ever knew, come on, get up now.

SEX AND DEATH 25

MAX. No, I have, I have. Wandering from one woman to the next like some primeval creature can't get its fill no matter how much it consumes! Sally. (*Puts his head in her lap.*)

SALLY. Are you crying? Are you crying, Maxwell?

MAX. (*Looks up into her face.*) Am I lost? Am I?

SALLY. Hush—honey—don't worry—Maxwell, darlin'—I'll save you!

(*LIGHTS down.*)

(*LIGHTS up.*)

Scene 2
The Living Room

MAXWELL speaks on the phone.

MAX. ... I'm in love! This time is different, I'm really in love, I haven't felt like this since ... high school. Sally. Sally! Is that a name? Sally Pinetree, does that fairly sing, I'm surprised they didn't stop her at the bridge and send her back! ... Twenty-two. I knew you'd say that, she's mature, wise even, wise as the hills, wise in a completely innocent, completely naive way. I don't know if *you'd* find her interesting, there are maybe three people in the world *you* find interesting and they all hang out at Raoul's after 2 AM. She's beautiful. Healthy beautiful, not like you New York City women think a frown's the final stamp of feminine loveliness, no. Sabrina, this woman is different from any woman I've ever met in my life, she's like a lake in the country. Georgia. Georgia, down south. Yes, she does. And she's always talking about her daddy, my daddy says this, my daddy says that, it drives me wild! ... Stop it. No. Sabrina. She's only had one lover before me and he was a Baptist, a Southern Baptist, the women's pure. Not like you, you slut. (*Laughs.*) I can't. I can't. I *can't*. Not even on the phone. (*Laughing, excited.*) Stop it, I'm not listening. You would? I know you would. I'd like to— (*Stops himself.*) Sabrina, stop. Stop! I mean it (*Fervently.*) I want to be true to Sally. Yes, all day. (*Pause.*) I called to ask you a favor. A great favor. Sally's birthday's coming up Friday, will you help me pick out a gift for her? (*Pause.*) Yes I did, I got you a candle snuffer, don't you remember, you used it as a pinky ring. Besides, our relationship was entirely—I know what *you'd* like but this is a different kind of— Please, you're the only one I can ask ... Something that'll make her happy, I depend on you, Sabrina ...

(*LIGHTS down.*)

(*LIGHTS up.*)

Scene 3
The Bedroom

SALLY and MAXWELL sit on the edge of the bed. MAXWELL presents SALLY with a wrapped box.

SALLY. For me?
MAX. Open it.
SALLY. I'm just all aquiver.
MAX. Open it.

SALLY. (*Unwraps the gift.*) I love presents! As a child, I'd open 'em and then I'd pack 'em up and re-open 'em again ... I'd save the wrapping! Keep it in the back of my closet, my daddy said, he said, Sally, why you holding onto them scraps of paper and I said, I said, Daddy, this was when you and momma gimme that set of teacups, this was when Aunt Martha gimme that bow for my hair, this— (*SHE has opened the gift. It's lingerie.*) Why.

MAX. Do you like it?

SALLY. Well I'm, I'm sure I do (*Puts it back in the box.*) I will cherish it forever. (*Closes the box.*)

MAX. Will you wear it?

SALLY. No.

MAX. Well, sweetheart ... l would like you to wear it. Without a woman, lingerie is just cloth ... Here, take it out.

SALLY. No.

MAX. Just take it out.

SALLY. No.

MAX. You hardly looked at it.

SALLY. I saw it.

MAX. It's one hundred percent silk.

SALLY. That's very nice, but honey, I—

MAX. (*Gets the lingerie out of the box, holds it up.*) Let me just hold it up against you—

SALLY. No!

MAX. I just want to see if the color suits you.

SALLY. No, I won't.

MAX. Okay, forget it. (*Flings the lingerie onto the bed, stands with his back to her.*)

SALLY. Maxwell? Honey? (*Goes to him.*) Now, don't be mad.

MAX. I brought you a present.

SALLY. Now that present wasn't for me, honey.

MAX. Who was it for?

SALLY. You. I don't wear things like that. Maxwell?

MAX. Did I ever tell you I hate it when you call me Maxwell?

SALLY. Max. Honey. Hush now, honey, don't get your skitters up; sweetheart, where I come from girls don't wear things like that. Not nice girls.

MAX. I bet your mother wears things like that for your father.

SALLY. My mother weighs two hundred pounds.

MAX. Your mother weighs two hundred pounds?

SALLY. That's right.

MAX. And your father stays with that?

SALLY. Please do not call momma "that." My daddy stays with momma, my daddy loves momma for who she is.

MAX. That's a big love.

SALLY. Sometimes I think you don't understand the nature of love, like the way you talk about the United States.

MAX. The United—?

SALLY. Always criticizing. Daddy told me everybody in New York City's always criticizing the United States, they can't even keep their streets clean, but they think they got the right to go 'round positively lambasting their own country ...When you love something you gotta love it with all its faults, not in spite of its faults but with its faults, because that's what makes it it.

MAX. You're teaching me the nature of love?

SALLY. I just thought you might like to hear another viewpoint—

MAX. You are twenty-two years old, I am thirty-eight, you're teaching me the nature of love—

SALLY. Everybody has a little something to learn—

MAX. I have made eighteen movies about love, you have gotten coffee and fetched sandwiches, and you are teaching me—

SALLY. You wanted me to save you!

(*This cuts through the argument.*)

MAX. Sally! Forgive me! You see? You see how I start reducing you, making you like other women? Forgive me. (*Embraces her.*) From now on, I'll bring you nothing but white cotton underpants. And white cotton bras. The kind General Robert E. Lee would sanction. The kind (*HE puts his hand up under her blouse and undoes her bra.*) that come undone.

(*THEY kiss.*)

(*LIGHTS down.*)

(*LIGHTS up.*)

Scene 4
The Living Room

MAXWELL is on the phone.

MAX. When did you first wear lingerie? ... You were not born with it. There must've been a point when you said to yourself, I am going to wear that, and you put it on for the first time. (*She is telling her story.*) You tramp ... You vixen ... You tart, I wish it'd been me. Am I being unfaithful to Sally if I picture you like that? (*Closes his eyes.*) It had little snaps where? Jesus. Stop it. You're so goddamn hot, baby, I'd love to take my tongue and wrap it around your hot pulsing—(*Stops himself.*) Sabrina. Please.

Stop. You're the only person I can talk to about this ... the whole thing was zippers! Stop! I'm trying to be a good man for the first time in my whole goddamn life, and you're not helping. What? I said, "I'm trying to be—" Good man. Good man. You have too heard of it. (*Just listens into the receiver; she is talking dirty to him.*) You know what I miss? You know what I really miss? Guess ... Mm hmm, I miss that. I miss that. I do miss that ... That. (*She's describing what he misses most.*) —Stop! Stop. We are friends, Sabrina. I'm not drumming it in, I'm just saying, we are friends! We've always been friends, but now we are *just* friends. I'm not drumming it in, I know I said it, but it has to be clear ... I know that. You never made demands. I'm not putting you in that class at all. Please let's not fight, I need you now, Sabrina, I need your help. (*Pauses, then launches on.*) How can I get Sally to wear lingerie? Please help me come up with a plan ... something subtle. Something that won't injure her sensibilities, she's just a kid—

(*LIGHTS down.*)

(*LIGHTS up.*)

Scene 5
The Bedroom

SALLY sits on the edge of the bed. Enter MAXWELL, wearing lingerie and high heels.

MAX. See?
SALLY. You look silly.
MAX. See, though?
SALLY. (*Laughing.*) You're making a spectacle of yourself.

MAX. Costume. Sheer costume. Nothing but a garment, a thin veneer of fabric over the man within. (*Looks at self in mirror.*) Not bad. (*Woman's voice.*) Ooooh! Oooh! Don't do that, you naughty fiend!

SALLY. Take that thing off and let's eat. I'm starving.

MAX. We just ate.

SALLY. I cannot subsist on sushi and watermelon sherbet, honey, I'm a healthy American woman.

MAX. (*Woman's voice.*) Oooooooh, you hulking ape!

SALLY. (*Alarmed.*) Are you homosexual?

MAX. (*Laughs.*) Baby, you are so susceptible, so gullible, that's why I love you. (*Sits beside her.*)

(*SHE puts her hand on his knee, HE slaps it.*)

MAX. Fresh! What kind of girl do you think I am?

SALLY. But you see it does change you, it does affect you.

MAX. How?

SALLY. It makes you into a bimbo.

MAX. I beg your pardon! Shall we discuss the use of cave symbolism in Fellini?

SALLY. But you can't discuss in that outfit, that outfit is totally incongruous with any intelligent discussion.

MAX. (*Momentarily nonplussed. Rises.*) But that's not what this outfit is for! This outfit is for lust! (*Peels off the lingerie, underneath which he is wearing very little; kneels at her feet; holds the lingerie out to her like an offering.*) This outfit is for ... admiring the white skin of your shoulder traversed by a single ribbon. Watching the blue veins of your breast pulsing against black lace. Stroking your hair falling over red silk. There's more to sex than kissing and feeling and fucking. There's presentation, there's gestalt, there's fantasy ... Sally. Please. Understand me. I see things. I live through my eyes. That's why I'm

an artist, that's why I make movies. I need to see you ...
my beloved ... my angel ... in this ... bless me with that
sight ... inspire me to create a love scene that will open the
gates of heaven and hell. Please.

SALLY. I couldn't. I wouldn't feel like myself.

MAX. So you'd feel like somebody else. Somebody
new, somebody exciting. Every new experience is part of
God's plan.

SALLY. Please don't bring God into this.

MAX. God made lingerie.

SALLY. He did not. Men made lingerie. Men who
don't respect women.

MAX. Sally. I love you. I want to marry you—

SALLY. You do?

MAX. Yes, some day. How could I respect you
anymore than I do? I exalt you, I worship you. Please.
Wear it for me. (*Sits beside her. strokes her hair.*) Every
morning, my dad left home for work, my mom would walk
him to the door. Every morning my dad would lean down
for a kiss and my mom would turn her face away. Every
goddamn morning. He'd leave a slightly more shrunken
man and she'd walk into the house into us kids with one
more of her nasty little triumphs—one day I asked her,
Mom, why don't you just kiss dad? She said, it isn't my
nature to show unnecessary affection, Maxwell.
Unnecessary affection. How can there be such a thing as
unnecessary affection? All affection is necessary—

SALLY. But your dad should've respected her and left
her alone. He was criticizing her.

MAX. My dad never criticized her, he was terrified of
her—

SALLY. Yes, he was! Every morning when he leaned
down for his kiss he was criticizing your mother! ... He
knew she wouldn't do it, and he was reminding her over
and over of his dissatisfaction ... Please. Take that thing

away. Throw it away. Let's get on with our life. We have a chance for something very beautiful together.

(*LIGHTS down.*)

(*LIGHTS up.*)

Scene 6
The Living Room

MAXWELL is on the phone.

MAX. I don't know if I can go the rest of my life without ever again seeing a woman in lingerie.

(*LIGHTS down.*)

(*LIGHTS up.*)

Scene 7
The Park

A pale harvest MOON hangs in the heavens, partly obscured by clouds. SALLY is waiting on the bench. Enter SABRINA.

SABRINA. Are you Sally?
SALLY. Yes.
SABRINA. Hello, my name's Sabrina. I'm a friend of Max Minsky. (*Reaches out hand.*)
SALLY. (*Shakes her hand.*) Where's Max?

SABRINA. He asked me to come.
SALLY. Is he ill?
SABRINA. Can we sit down?
SALLY. Yes.

(*THEY sit. SABRINA examines Sally.*)

SALLY. Excuse me. Is there something wrong?
SABRINA. Sorry, it's just I've heard so much about you these past three months, you are exactly as I expected.
SALLY. What did you expect?
SABRINA. You.
SALLY. You haven't told me where Max is.
SABRINA. He's not coming. Don't worry! He's fine, just ... upset. I've know Max for four years.
SALLY. Is that right?
SABRINA. Yes. I tell him things from the woman's point of view, he tells me things from the man's point of view, helps cast some light on the strange, inexplicable behavior of the male species.
SALLY. You know— All the single women I meet, I've only been here six months but all the single women I meet in New York City, they are all so down on men. I don't agree. Where I come from there are many very good men, my own father among them—
SABRINA. I'm not down on men! I love men! I don't claim to understand them, that's all.
SALLY. Where is Max?
SABRINA. Max asked me to tell you that he loves you very much and couldn't come because he needs time to think.
SALLY. Time to think—?
SABRINA. Just one night.
SALLY. Where did he tell you this?
SABRINA. Just—a few minutes ago—

SALLY. Where?

SABRINA. Where?

SALLY. Were you in his apartment?

SABRINA. Over the telephone.

SALLY. You weren't with him?

SABRINA. No. I told you. We're just friends.

SALLY. You're awfully pretty to be just friends.

SABRINA. There are a lot of pretty women in this town ... You really love him, don't you?

SALLY. I've never felt like this before in my entire life, I think about him day and night, I dream about him, I want him so much I could choke—yes. I love him.

SABRINA. There's something you should know.

SALLY. I beg your pardon?

SABRINA. There's something you should know.

SALLY. He's going away with you!

SABRINA. No! I tell you, we are just friends. Something you should know about Max.

SALLY. He's ill—

SABRINA. No. This is something Max himself does not know. Only I know it. And perhaps other women he has ... been close with. Has Max told you about his past?

SALLY. Blow by blow, I know everything—

SABRINA. Everything. And his past with women?

SALLY. I know everything.

SABRINA. How he hurts them?

SALLY. I know all about it.

SABRINA. How he's gone through the women of this city like a sickle through spring grass? He's a dangerous man.

SALLY. Not to me.

SABRINA. Not to you. What do you think makes a man dangerous to women? I'll tell you. To the extent a man does not know himself, to that extent he is dangerous to women. Max Minsky is a very dangerous man to women. Because there's something he does not know about himself ...

SALLY. He knows he has trouble making a commitment, he's very aware of that, my love will save him—

SABRINA. (*Laughs involuntarily.*) Honey, you are sweet. Please. Try to save the starving hordes of Ethiopia. Don't try to save a man. Listen. Max Minsky doesn't know ... that he can't respect any woman he enjoys fucking. Hush. Just listen. If a woman's really hot in bed Max puts her in a category—

SALLY. How do you know?

SABRINA. Just listen! I'm trying to help you. I'm on your side. Will you listen?

SALLY. Go on.

SABRINA. Don't wear that lingerie.

SALLY. The lingerie—

SABRINA. The lingerie Max keeps pushing on you. Don't wear it. No matter what you do, don't wear it. Right now he sees you as the Madonna. You hold out long enough he'll marry you. Listen to me! But if you don't hold out ... He'll make out like he wants you to wear that lingerie like his life depends on it but when you do he'll discard you—

SALLY. Discard me?

SABRINA. He wants you to be a whore so he can discard you. He doesn't know this about himself.

SALLY. I'm no whore—

SABRINA. I know that! You're a beautiful, sweet, wholesome girl who could make Max Minsky very happy. I'd like Max to be happy—

SALLY. Why?

SABRINA. I told you! I'm his friend.

SALLY. But you're not my friend. I don't even know you. Why should I trust you?

SABRINA. (*Laughs.*) I'm the one who told Max to get that lingerie in the first place, I shopped with him ... it was a little joke ... I know him so well, I knew what it would do—

SALLY. Make him hate me?

SABRINA. Make him see himself, maybe—

SALLY. You love Max!

SABRINA. ... Yes. I suppose I love Max. I suppose I'll always love Max. But so what? Max can never love me. I wear lingerie.

SALLY. You must think we southern girls are pretty gullible.

(*LIGHTS down.*)

(*LIGHTS up.*)

Scene 8
The Bedroom

MAXWELL is pacing. SALLY sits on the bed.

MAX. Either you do or you don't. That's all! It's as simple as that. No! I'm not listening to any more arguments. If you love me like you say you do, you put on that lingerie for me. That's all. No! No more arguments. I don't want to hear about your momma and your daddy and God and self respect and rotten commies, we're talking something very real here, very real, loving someone, caring about him enough to want to make him happy. No! I'm not listening. I've tried everything. Reasoning, pleading, cajoling, dressing up like a tart, I've tried it all, I'm not asking you to jump off a cliff, I'm asking you to put on a piece of clothing for me, that's all, if you don't love me enough for that what the hell's gonna happen when something really important comes up! I'll be desperate, you'll be singing the National Anthem, no! No, Sally! There isn't anything more to say! There's the lingerie. There's the champagne. Drink a glass of champagne, put on the lingerie and be a woman to your man, be a woman to your man, take a chance for your man, it's not a lot to ask, it's nothing to ask, no! Sally, if you can't do this much for me, yes, for me, I admit, for me, it's true, for me, okay, for me, what's wrong with that, for me, isn't that love? That we do things for each other? Then I can't stay with you. I'm too vulnerable. I can't trust you to sacrifice for me at all ever, I'm out of here.

SALLY. Pour me a glass of champagne.

(*MAX pours champagne; SHE drinks it, stands, takes the bottle of champagne and the lingerie, heads toward the bathroom.*)

SALLY. Maxwell—Max—would you marry a woman who wears lingerie?

MAX. I would never marry a woman who doesn't.

(*LIGHTS down.*)

(*LIGHTS up.*)

Scene 9
The Bedroom

MAXWELL is sprawled on the bed, smoking, reading a magazine. HE has just finished making love and is tousled, rosy, content.

MAX. (*Toward the bathroom.*) Baby! Baby! Did I thank you, baby? Did I thank you for reminding me why I'm alive! Thank you! Thank you, baby! Come back here. I got something for you. It's in my pants. Actually, my pants are on the floor, if it's in my pants I'm in a lot of trouble. (*Checks himself.*) I got it! I got it right here! I'm keeping it warm for you, baby! Are you taking it off? Don't take it off! Let me see you! Let me see you in it! One more time! My eyes are still hungry, baby! Baby! Come out! Come out, baby! Come to daddy! (*A ray of LIGHT from offstage; the bathroom door has opened.*)

(*Enter SABRINA, wearing lingerie. SHE is tousled, rosy, content.*)

MAX. Stop right there. I just want to look at you.

(*SABRINA does a little snake dance, turns around, sticks her butt toward him, a bump and grind. She is very sexy. THEY laugh.*)

MAX. You are the hottest piece of ass I've ever had the good fortune to fuck my brains out with. (*SHE tumbles into his arms and THEY kiss, open-mouthed, passionately.*) How come you keep turning up in my bed? How do you do that?
SABRINA. Bad habit. (*THEY kiss. Referring to her lingerie.*) How did you get this away from her?

MAX. Who?

SABRINA. Sally. Sally Pinetree. Isn't this the same lingerie you gave to that sweet young innocent Sally Pinetree?

MAX. She may've been young. (*Kisses her.*) But she wasn't so sweet. (*Kisses her.*) And she wasn't so innocent. (*Kisses her.*) And it looks a thousand times better on you. And it feels a thousand times better on you. And it smells a thousand times better on you. And it tastes—(*He bites her, SHE squeals.*)

SABRINA. Did she give it back to you?

MAX. I can't even think about her when I'm with you.

SABRINA. Let's go for a ride! In a —I know! In a hansom cab. Through Central Park together!

MAX. Now?

SABRINA. Right now. A romantic ride through Central Park, just the two of ... we can fuck in the back. Nobody'd notice a little extra bouncing.

MAX. I can't tonight, Sabrina. I gotta work, I gotta edit, I told you that. (*Kisses her softly.*) You have to go home.

SABRINA. Hey! That's fine. That's okay. (*Exiting.*) No agendas. No programs.

MAX. God, I love lingerie.

(*LIGHTS down.*)

CURTAIN

COSTUME PLOT

Scene 1	Max	Trendy suit, double-breasted
	Sally	Simple sun dress
Scene 2	Max	Sweatsuit and sneakers
	Sally	Flannel nightie, ankle length, long sleeves, white
Scene 4	Max	Same as 3
Scene 5	Max	Lingerie, boxer shorts
	Sally	Day dress (can be same as worn in Sc. 1)
Scene 6	Max	Robe or smoking jacket, long
Scene 7	Sabrina	Flashy (but not tacky) blouse, tight pants, flats
	Sally	Day dress
Scene 8	Max	Evening wear, rumpled
	Sally	Evening dress

Scene 9	Sabrina	Lingerie, stocking with garters, heels
	Max	wrapped in bed sheet

This costume plot is offered merely as a guideline to suggest times of day and passage of time. The play will work as well if the actors wear the same costumes for each scene.

PROPERTY LIST

<u>Furniture and furnishings</u>

Park bench
Bed with linens
Bookcase
Shrub/tree for park area
Curtains for bedroom window
Chair
Telephone stand
Telephone

<u>Other Props</u>

Wrapped gift box (Max, Sc. 3) containing lingerie
Lingerie (Max, Sabrina, Sc. 3,5,8 and 9)
Cigarettes (Sabrina, Sc. 7)
Bottle of Champagne (Max and Sally, Sc. 8)
Champagne buckets with ice (Max, Sally, Sc. 8)
2 Champagne flutes (Max, Sally, Sc. 8)

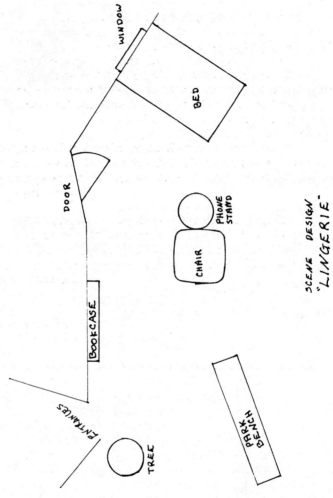

SCENE DESIGN
"LINGERIE"

MILK

A one-act drama

CHARACTERS

RYAN (late twenties)
JILL (late twenties)
RYAN II (late teens)
JILL II (late teens)
BARRY (around forty)
SAUL (around forty-five)
LILA (around sixty)

Time: The Present

SETTING: Composite set, representing a bedroom, a subway car, an airport runway and a business with conference table.

MILK

LIGHTS up on a space. RYAN and JILL are fighting. This fight is somewhere between a debate and a boxing match, delivering blows with words.

RYAN. The gods that sleep in museums: the god of fire with his incense burner that resembles an Inquisition tripod; Tlaloc, one of the manifold Gods of the Waters, on his wall of green granite ...

(Overlapping.)

JILL. Meat ... Bread ... Crumbs ...

RYAN. ... The Mother Goddess of Waters, the Mother Goddess of Flowers; the immutable expression, echoing from beneath many layers of water, of the Goddess robed in green jade; the enraptured, blissful expression ...

JILL. ... Couch ... Hands ... Hand lotion ...

RYAN. ... Features crackling with incense, where atoms of sunlight circle—the countenance of the Mother Goddess of Flowers; this world of obligatory servitude in which a stone comes alive ...

JILL. ... Hand cream ... Rubber gloves ... Spout ...

RYAN. ... the world of organically civilized men whose vital organs too awaken from their slumber, this human world enters into us ...

(The ROAR of the crowd is heard, grows.)

JILL. Water! Dishes! Forks! Spoons! Knives! Soap! Soap suds! Vitamins! Eye dropper! Mouth!

RYAN. ... participating in the dance of the gods without turning 'round or looking back, on pain of becoming, like ourselves, crumbled pillars of salt ...

(*The ROAR of the crowd.*)

JILL. Telephone! Refrigerator! Magnets! Shelves! Vitamins!

(*A BUZZER.*)

JILL. (*Becoming uncertain.*) ... Eye dropper ... Mouth ... Teeth ...
RYAN. (*Gaining strength.*) How hard it is! When everything encourages us to sleep! Though we may look about us! With clinging, conscious eyes! To wake!

JILL. .... Breast ... Nipple ...Nipple ...

(*The BUZZER.*)

JILL. ... Breast ...

(*The BUZZER.*)

JILL. No. No. Cookies? Rocks? Pebbles? Stones?

(*The ROAR of the crowd rises, until it becomes clear that they are chanting: Ryan, Ryan, Ryan, Ryan, Ryan, Ryan, Ryan etc.*)

RYAN. And yet look about us! As in a dream! With eyes that no longer know their function and whose gaze is turned inward, look! Look!

(BLACKOUT.
The ROAR of the crowd: Ryan, Ryan, Ryan, Ryan,
builds, then is cut off.
LIGHTS up on Ryan and Jill's bedroom. Early morning.
RYAN sleeps.
Enter JILL in functional pajamas, putting her breast away.
She has been nursing. SHE looks exhausted.)

JILL. (*Looking at Ryan.*) Christ. (*Waking him.*) Ryan.
Rye! Ryan. Ryan! Rise and shine! New day! Up up up up
up!

(RYAN does not wake up. JILL contemplates her side of
the bed, and climbs in. As she lies there, SHE speaks to
Ryan.)

JILL. Rye! Ryan! You have to get up. You have to go
to work. (*SHE shakes him. Reminding him of things.*)
Lila! Saul! Uncle Barry! The mission statement! It's
twenty after. Rye!

RYAN. Okay, okay, minute.

(JILL cannot resist the pillow, gives up, falls asleep.
THEY both sleep, backs turned to each other.
A BABY cries, offstage.
JILL rouses, wakes. The BABY's crying becomes louder.
JILL gets an alarm clock, triggers it, and puts it near
Ryan.
Exit JILL toward the crying baby.
The ALARM CLOCK continues to ring.
BLACKOUT.
LIGHTS up on an airport runway. RYAN II and JILL II lie
on the runway, looking up. THEY are absolutely still
for a long time. There is no sound or movement.

LIGHTS up on a subway car. RYAN, in business attire, is straphanging. Through the window of the subway car, HE watches RYAN II and JILL II on the runway.
There is the sound of a MACHINE coming. Getting louder and louder. Then the huge bursting, overpowering roar of an AIRPLANE going up and a black SHADOW, an extraordinary vibration passes over RYAN II and JILL II, very close.
THEY hold hands and laugh, shudder, hold each other, kiss, laugh.
RYAN laughs, watching, from the subway car.)

JILL II. (*Sits up and speaks to Ryan.*) Don't go to work. Your mind is withering away. Your soul is being corrupted. You mustn't go to work. I forbid it! Go right on to Coney Island ... Right on to Coney Island ... Right on to Coney Island ...

(*LIGHTS up on a conference table. LILA, SAUL, and BARRY, in business attire, sit around the table. THEY are looking at documents, sipping coffee.*
JILL II' s voice fades.
The runway fades.
BLACKOUT on RYAN, RYAN II and JILL II.)

BARRY. (*Reading from a sheet of loose paper.*) "These capabilities result in implementable short and long term solutions that make the most effective use of available resources. Our consultants are comfortable working in unstructured environments and with a minimum of supervision. The single factor which infuses all our business dealings, however, can be summed up in just a few words: we care about the individual."
LILA. Would you mind reading that last line one more time? Thank you.

(*Enter RYAN. HE takes his place at the table. The OTHERS completely ignore him.*)

BARRY. The single factor which infuses all our business dealings, however, can be summed up in just a few words: we care about the individual.

LILA. We're very close.

BARRY. Very close.

LILA. But that last line. What do you think of it, Barry?

BARRY. I'd like to hear what you think of it, Lila.

SAUL. I think, I think, I think we're very close, but that there's something not just exactly on the button yet about that there, Lila.

LILA. I think you're right. We care about the individual. (*Pause.*) No. Not right.

(*THEY all consider the gravity of the situation.*)

RYAN. What don't you like about it?

(*THEY all ignore him.*)

LILA. Is there another way of saying it?

(*THEY all think about it.*)

SAUL. Wait, here, okay, can I just write? I just would like to write, because otherwise, it's in one ear—(*HE writes,* then reads what he has written.) We are concerned with each and every one of our clients.

LILA. Good writing is short, not long. Can we cut the sentence down? We care about the individual. Five words. Can we cut the sentence down?

(*THEY all think about it.*)

   RYAN. No.
   LILA. Good morning, Ryan.
   RYAN. Good morning. Sorry. The baby was up all night—
   LILA. We know, we had a call from your wife, lovely girl—All right. We believe that we can cut the sentence down. "We care about the individual." Five words.

(*THEY all think about it.*)

   BARRY. We facilitate the individual. Four words. We impact the individual. Four words. We involve the individual. Four words.
   SAUL. We facilitate individuals. Three words. We impact individuals. Three words. We—what was it—involve individuals. Three words.
   LILA. Interesting.
   SAUL. Because, you know, when, when you're talking about individuals, right, it's gotta be better to say more than one.
   LILA. What do you think, Ryan? You are the wordsmith.
   RYAN. I think the entire passage has ceased to have any meaning. We've tinkered with it so much, it's lost all life.

(*THEY all stare at him.*)

   BARRY. (*Slaps Ryan on the back.*) Always the philosopher! We're very close.
   SAUL. (*To Ryan.*) Jesus, next time come about an hour later. (*Laughs.*)

(*NOBODY else laughs.*)

LILA. "Involve." A good, strong word. We involve the individual. Try it. Read it to me. Ryan.

(*BLACKOUT.*
LIGHTS up on the subway.
RYAN and BARRY are straphanging.
During the following, LIGHTS rise and blackout, rise and
    blackout, on RYAN II and JILL II, lying on the
    runway. RYAN watches them intently through the
    black glass of the subway car.)

BARRY. ... It's how we package it, packaging is ninety percent, I'm telling you, we could write "See the Purple Monkey Fuck the Orange Baboon" and if you package it right, glossy, high-class, varnished, photos, four-color, because nobody reads the damn copy anyway, all they want, all they're looking for, is flash. Image. Image. Can they do business with your business? One look they made up their mind. You just got to placate Lila, that's all, it's her company, she can't face up that it doesn't matter a fig whether the word is—Where are you?

RYAN. Sorry. I was just—what were you saying?

BARRY. What's on your mind, Ryan?

RYAN. I was just remembering how I met Jill.

BARRY. That's what you're thinking about?

RYAN. I guess it's the sound—the subway— Did you know that Jill used to go to the Anchorage Airport and lie out on the runway.

BARRY. What for?

RYAN. One night, I was just wandering there, wandering through the fields, actually—

BARRY. What, were you drinking?

RYAN. What? No, no—wandering—looking at the stars, you know, I came upon this highway, I thought, strange, no cars, and then I see this girl—just lying there— in the middle of the road. Her hair spread out over the concrete.

BARRY. Who was that?

RYAN. Jill.

(*Together:*)

BARRY. Your wife?   RYAN. And then I hear
                                                        something.

RYAN. I look down the road ... out of the mist, the nose of a giant bird, silver, shining, alien, bearing down on her—I tumbled down beside her, rolled with her out of the way just as the belly of the bird roared over us—It was an airplane. She had very long hair then, long. Below her knees.

BARRY. You know. You're too serious. That's your problem. Your mother was the same way. Gotta lighten up, kid—

RYAN. And now she's cut it all off.

(*Long beat.*)

BARRY. (*Regards Ryan.*) You need a woman.

RYAN. What?

(*Together:*)

BARRY. A woman, you   RYAN. What are you
need a woman.   talking about?

RYAN. I'm married.

BARRY. That has nothing to do with it. I've been trying to figure out what's bugging you at work—

Sometimes I think you're asking to get kicked out on your ass— Do you know what I had to go through to get you that job? And you've been acting strange—

RYAN. I've been acting—

BARRY. Yes, strange. Strange. Late every other morning. Distracted. Disrespectful—

(*Overlapping:*)

RYAN. I'm not disrespectful ... I just want to tell the truth ... You can put up with it... I can't put up with it ...	BARRY. Disrespectful, yes. You are. The truth? You know the truth? You got a personal license to the truth?

BARRY. Come down from the ivory tower, Rapunzel, and meet the real world! Wife. Child. Job. Boss. Alarm clock goes off, you gotta get up! Up! Look, kid. You're going through a very hard time. A lot of marriages don't even make it. A woman. Just to get you through the slump.

RYAN. Uncle Barry, I'm crazy in love with my wife—

BARRY. Yeah? And who's she in love with? You? Or that baby?

(*BLACKOUT.*
(*LIGHTS up on Ryan and Jill's bedroom. Evening. JILL is sitting in the rocking chair, rocking, nursing the baby. RYAN paces like a caged animal. HE is drinking scotch out of the bottle.*)

RYAN. Okay, look look look. Jill. I'll get a teaching job.

JILL. We tried that! There's not one decent opening all up and down the east coast, let's face it, we studied the wrong thing. (*Contemptuously.*) Philosophy!

RYAN. There was that job in Illinois—

JILL. Twelve hundred dollars a semester. Can we live on twelve hundred dollars a semester? We can't even live on what you're making now, with all the debts.

RYAN. We used to live on nothing—

JILL. We have a baby now! (*Pause.*) Rye. If she gets a cold. If anything happens. We can't just uproot—We're not children anymore. I'm sorry. I can't help it. I want a home.

RYAN. (*Kneeling at her feet.*) Antonin Artaud.

JILL. Oh, Rye—

RYAN. (*Quoting from memory, with great passion.*) Furthermore, when we speak of life, it must be understood that we are not referring to life as we know it from its surface of fact, but to that fragile, fluctuating center which forms never reach. And if there is still one hellish, truly accursed thing in our time, it is our artistic dallying with forms, instead of being like victims burnt at the stake, signalling through the flames!

JILL. (*To the baby, with infinite tenderness.*) Ow, not so hard.

RYAN. (*Stands.*) You're not even listening to me!

JILL. I'm sorry, she grabbed me wrong—My breast is still a little sore—They're beautiful words.

RYAN. Beautiful words? We used to live by these words, we used to eat, drink and make love by these words and Norman Brown, Kapleau—

JILL. Yes, I know, I know, don't get so upset—

RYAN. We had something, the two of us, we were not going to succumb to the petty details of existence, we were not going to be clipped and dried and sucked of everything like the rest of them—like—like Saul—Do you want me to end up like Saul?

JILL. Saul?

RYAN. Saul from the office, I've told you about him twenty-five times, do you ever listen to anything I say to you anymore?

JILL. Saul. All right, Saul. Yes, I remember now. He used to be the company's ace salesman. And now he's pathetic.

RYAN. Is that how you want me to end up?

JILL. Honey—

RYAN. Because that's what I will end up if I stay there, Jill, pathetic! I will be pathetic! I will learn to cover and quake, I will learn to despise the truth to save my ass!

JILL. Okay. Can you sit down? She isn't nursing right. She feels your anger. Please. Sit down.

(*RYAN sits on the bed, swigs from the bottle.*)

JILL. (*Referring to his drinking.*) You won't want to get up in the morning. How many times can I call them and blame it on the baby? I'm sorry. All right. Honey. I know it's killing you, that job. I see how you shrink when you go in, how you toss all night. What can I say, you—

RYAN. Well for one thing you could say that I—

JILL. Just wait, wait, wait, just let me finish. Okay? We have a child now.

RYAN. You always say that, like it says everything, like it—

JILL. Wait, wait. Okay. Being with the baby. I don't really have the time to think anymore, my brain is kinda— foggy. (*Composes her thought.*) Everybody has to give up things, Rye. Only children or rich people or very very very selfish people can have or even want to have everything just the way they want to. Don't you think—for instance, this is small—but don't you think I'd like to have a slug of that scotch? But I can't. I haven't had a drink in a year and a half.

RYAN. (*Holds out the scotch to her.*) Go on. Let's have one drink together. One fucking drink together!

(*Beat.*)

JILL. Okay. (*Reaches for the bottle.*)
RYAN. No! (*Stops her.*) Your milk.

(*BLACKOUT.*
Bed. The middle of the night.
RYAN and JILL are sleeping.
A BABY cries, offstage.
RYAN continues to sleep soundly, but JILL stirs, rises, exits towards the crying baby.
Enter JILL II, naked or dressed in a transparent, mythic dress.)

RYAN. Are you the one?
JILL II. Shhh. (*She puts his hand on her breast.*) The breasts of a girl. Empty. Innocent. Lush.
RYAN. I am going to fuck you. I am going to fuck you so hard you won't breathe, I am enormous, I am going to come in you—

(*Enter JILL. Exit JILL II.*
RYAN is suddenly quiet, sleeping.
JILL gets into bed, and looks at him with great tenderness. SHE lies down beside him and HE reaches for her, hungrily.)

JILL. Please, let me sleep. (*Turns away from him.*) I love you. (*Falls asleep instantly.*)

(*RYAN, eyes open, rolls over and looks into the darkness. BLACKOUT.*)

LILA. (*Her voice, cold, in the blackness.*) When you've been in the business a little longer, Ryan, you'll learn that there is a good reason for things to become clichés. They become clichés because they are true. Now. We are very, very close. Read me the passage again.

(*LIGHTS up on the conference table. RYAN, BARRY, LILA and SAUL.*
During this scene, LILA's mood is dark and impatient.)

RYAN. I just lost my place here—
BARRY. Paragraph 2, Ryan.
RYAN. "The single factor which infuses all our business dealings, however, can be summed up in just a few words: We involve the individual."
LILA. When did that change?
RYAN. Excuse me?
LILA. That last line. When did that change?

(*THEY all stare at Ryan.*)

RYAN. Are you asking me when I changed this?
LILA. I think that's what I said, yes.
RYAN. Yesterday. After our meeting.
LILA. What was it before? Saul, ring Betsy for me, would you, please? Not that phone. Use that phone. Yes. What was it before?
RYAN. What was it before?
BARRY. It was: We care about the individual. Here. Here it is. (*Presents Lila with a piece of paper.*)
LILA. (*To Saul.*) Did you get her?
SAUL. You know, now I know this is a new system here, Lila, isn't it, isn't it funny keeping up with all these new systems—

LILA. (*Calls.*) Betsy! Betsy! Saul, go find her. Tell her I want a coffee black.

SAUL. You want me to go find—okay—Betsy? Is she your secretary now? I thought she was in R&D. Unless that's a different Betsy. (*Exits. Enters.*) Did you say? Maybe you can, well, I don't see her out there, I mean, isn't she, wouldn't she be, well, her desk is— I'll find her. (*Exits.*)

(*With a sigh of impatience, LILA goes to the phone and dials. While she is on the phone, BARRY hands Ryan a slip of paper. RYAN looks at it. It is the number of a woman.*)

LILA. Abigail. Is Betsy away from her desk again? I will not put up with her constant wanderings, if she wants to socialize tell her to get a job as a dancehall girl. Thank you. And get us some coffee in here. I called for it hours ago. Thank you.

BARRY. (*Confidentially.*) A little escape valve.

(*LILA returns to the table.*
RYAN holds the note in his hand.)

LILA. (*Reads.*) dadededumdedumdadedumde dumdedum can be summed up in just a few words: We care about the individual. (*Puts the paper down and looks at Ryan.*)

LILA. Why did you change this?

BARRY. He no doubt just—

LILA. Wait a minute now, Barry, I know he's your nephew but let the boy speak for himself. Why did you change this? (*Beat.*) Don't you know what the concept of "care" means to his organization? (*Beat.*) Have you read our principles of organization, Ryan?

RYAN. (*Crumples the note.*) Yes, of course I have, but you see, the reason I changed the word from "care" to "involve" is because you said to—

BARRY. (*Sharply interrupting.*) Sometimes the young are very impatient and restless, Lila, and it takes them awhile to learn how to just settle down. Just settle down. I know you understand that.

SAUL. (*Enters with the coffee.*) Okay, two black, one cream and sugar, sometime it don't matter V.P. or what you still got to do, do something yourself or it don't get—

LILA. Shh shh shh thank you, Saul. Thank you. (*Deeply inhales her coffee. SHE is calming down.*) Yes. All right. I was young once.

BARRY. You still are, Lila.

SAUL. You still are, Lila.

(*Beat.*)

RYAN. You still are.

(*BLACKOUT. LIGHTS up on the runway. Nighttime SOUNDS.*
RYAN II and JILL II are having a picnic. RYAN II is reading from a book.)

RYAN II. ... To wake and yet look about us as in a dream, with eyes that no longer know their function and whose gaze is turned inward.

JILL II. My God.

RYAN II. He's incredible, isn't he?

(*THEY kiss passionately.*)

JILL II. And yet—do you know the very very very strange thing about him? He himself advocated the burning of books!

RYAN II. Do you see that as a contradiction?

JILL II. Not at all. It is at the very heart of the entire issue of paradox. In the very act of destroying words, we fulfill them! Where is that passage? (*Takes up the book, finds a place.*) The library at Alexandria can be burnt down. There are forces above and beyond papyrus.

RYAN II. Papyrus—

JILL II. Paper. But listen, listen, listen. (*Reads.*) There are forces above and beyond papyrus. We may temporarily be deprived of our ability to discover these forces, but their energy will not be suppressed. (*Stands, finds a match, and lights the book on fire.*)

RYAN II. Jill—what are you doing?

(*JILL II laughs ecstatically.*)

RYAN II. Don't do that—What will I use for my term paper?

JILL II. This is your term paper!

(*LIGHTS up on the subway car. Through the black of the subway car window, RYAN watches RYAN II and JILL II, sadly, with nostalgia.*)

JILL II. (*Gives to Ryan II a sheet of burning paper.*) Here, here, here. We must always do everything together. We must always experience everything together.

RYAN II. But drop it—drop it—you'll burn your fingers—

BARRY. (*Comes up to Ryan in the subway car.*) Hey, kid.

(*Over the runway, there is the incredible vibration and the great wind of an AIRPLANE going close by overhead. The fire goes out.*)

RYAN. (*Disturbed from his reverie.*) Oh—Uncle Barry—

(*BLACKOUT the runway.*)

BARRY. (*Speaks to Ryan in the subway car.*) You look like your dead mother's out that window. Well, we finally got the Mission Statement put to bed. Tomorrow the Cold Calls Form. You gonna be there?

RYAN. Uncle Barry. You saw what happened. I was just trying to tell her—

BARRY. I know what you were trying to tell her. But she gets very touchy when employees point out her faults to her. Bosses are like that.

(*Overlapping:*)

RYAN.	BARRY.
But she doesn't remember what she says from one day to the next ... Is she senile? Is she crazy?	No, she's not senile ... No, she's not crazy ... That is her right ...

She constantly changes her mind ...

BARRY. That is her right! Lila Price has worked her whole life to build that business and she built it out of nothing, and now she gives three hundred people jobs, so if she wants to change her mind from time to time, that is her right, cookie. Lucky thing for you you're handsome and you look good in a suit. But not that handsome.

(*Beat.*)

RYAN. I can't use that phone number you gave me.
BARRY. Hey! That's fine! That's up to you! You got
it. You think it'll help you, use it. You don't, don't. Just
do what you gotta do to stop being a pain in my neck.

(*BLACKOUT.*
(*The bedroom. The middle of the night.*
JILL sleeps soundly.
*RYAN leans over her, just watching her. HE goes to touch
  her, but it is as if an invisible wall were around her,
  keeping his hand away. HE curls up and goes to sleep,
  his back to her.*
*Enter JILL II, naked or wearing a transparent, mythic
  gown. SHE carries a burning torch. SHE speaks and
  gestures ceremoniously.*)

JILL II. Sleeper, awake! Sleep is separateness, the cave
of solitude is the cave of dreams, to be awake is to
participate, carnally! And not in fantasy, in the feast! The
great communion!
RYAN. (*Seeing Jill II.*) Jill! Where have you been? I
thought you were dead! I thought you had disappeared one
night when we were wandering through the city, I turned
around and you were gone—but I couldn't remember
exactly where, exactly when—and the city suddenly seemed
strange, like a place I'd never seen before, I couldn't
remember the names of the streets, I couldn't remember
uptown from downtown, I had only a number to call, but I
couldn't remember where I had put the number, my pockets
were dangerously deep, I feared putting my hands into
them, there were lakes in them, and now you're—now—

(The sound of a BABY crying, offstage.)

RYAN. Quick—you better go—she'll wake up—

(JILL II points the torch toward the sound of the baby crying, and the BABY is quiet. The TORCH goes out. JILL II climbs into bed with Ryan and Jill. JILL II and RYAN begin to make love.)

RYAN. No ... Not here ... With her ...
JILL II. I am her.

(BLACKOUT.
LIGHTS up on the bedroom. Early morning.
RYAN II and JILL II are in bed, curled in each other's arms.
The ALARM CLOCK goes off.
RYAN II shuts it off, rises.)

RYAN II. I'd better go in to work.
JILL II. Don't go in to work.
RYAN II. But it's a very important day at work.
JILL II. Stay here with me.
RYAN II. They'll fire me.
JILL II. Good.
RYAN II. What about the baby?
JILL II. The baby is dead.

(BLACKOUT.
LIGHTS up on the conference table.
RYAN sits alone. HE looks very well-dressed, orderly, composed. HE is studying papers.
Enter LILA, BARRY and SAUL.)

SAUL. I know I for one, if I was doing this job, and I did do this job, I'd want more than two lines—

BARRY. (*Arguing with Saul.*) It's very simple. You say Office Manager. Assistant to the Office Manager. Secretary. Hell, all we're gonna get is goddamn secretaries anyway—

(*RYAN rises respectfully.*)

LILA. Well! Good morning, Ryan.
RYAN. Morning. Morning. Morning.
LILA. How's the baby?
RYAN. Fine. Just fine.
LILA. War is hell? Babies are hell.

(*THEY all laugh.*)

LILA. We've had a chance to look over your Cold Calls Form, Ryan, and I must congratulate you. We're close. Very close.
RYAN. Thank you.
SAUL. But I'm tellin' you, we need more than two lines—
BARRY. We don't need two lines.
SAUL. I know I for one if I was doing this job, I would want to write down what happened.
BARRY. What could happen, Saul?
SAUL. Like anything. Like call next week. Call next month. No interest. I'm tellin' you, sales, the whole point is the schmooze. You schmooze enough, you close the deal they don't even notice they bit.
BARRY. We are not selling encyclopedias here.
SAUL. Look it don't matter what the fuck you're selling, selling is selling—

BARRY. I agree with you, but we are not using this form to sell, Saul. This is just the entree. The getter in the door.

(*Beat.*)

SAUL. Okay. I'm not. I mean, okay. **Drop it.**
LILA. Saul, not so touchy—
SAUL. I'm not touchy, I'm just—well, you know, for God's sake, he—I mean Barry's been here awhile but (*Referring to Ryan.*) he—
LILA. I'm sure we all want to hear your opinion. You have more experience in sales than any of us.

(*Beat.*)

SAUL. Okay. You call Bridgeport. You get someone's sec, you give her the spiel, she says, I'm not the right person to talk to about this. You want Donovan in R&D. But to get Donovan in R&D, you got to go through Alice somebody in reception. Tell her that JoAnn sent you. That's about six lines.
BARRY. That's one line. Call Donovan, go through Alice, mention JoAnn, and the number. One line.
SAUL. How'd you get that, no, because it isn't.
BARRY. You can also spend four lines writing the address.

(*LILA laughs. THEY all laugh.*)

SAUL. Okay, look, I said drop it. One line, two lines, three lines, fuck, what does it matter?
LILA. It matters. (*Beat.*) You know it matters, Saul.
SAUL. That's what I'm saying, it matters. Lila, you, you've worked up down this business and everything in

between, you know what bozos they got out there, take some bozo, some kid doesn't even speak English, she don't know exactly which information to take down, give her three lines, she'll record everything, then the supervisor, I'm telling you, you'll get a lot more valuable information that way. Who-to. Where-to. When-to.

LILA. (*Pause.*) He's right.

(*Silence. Pause. This is a major victory for Saul.*)

BARRY. Okay. Fine. Three lines.
SAUL. I thank you. And my entire staff thanks you.
RYAN. No.

(*THEY all stare at Ryan.*)

RYAN. Excuse me, with all due respect, there are other considerations. Budget, for one. If you add another line you're going to have to add another page.

LILA. Another page? Two sheets per caller?

RYAN. Per call. Two sheets per call per caller.

LILA. That is out of the question. Saul, see if there's coffee. (*Pause.*) See if there's coffee.

SAUL. Okay. (*Stands, starts to exit, erupts.*) Who is this kid? Some snotnose brat, some blood relation barely got his thumb outta his mouth? And he's writing the Cold Calls Form? He's writing the Cold Calls Form? He's writing the Cold Calls Form? Is this kid the kind of person you want at Price now, Lila? Cause if it is, I think you're forgetting what the fuck this company is all about, I think you're —

LILA. Stop it. (*Silence.*) Ryan. See if there's coffee.

(*BLACKOUT.*

*LIGHTS up on the bedroom. Early evening. The PHONE
rings Enter RYAN, holding the baby. HE picks up the
phone.)*

RYAN. *(Into the phone.)* Oh—hi. I'm very sorry. Yes,
I heard about it. I said I'm sorry. I am sorry. I'm really
sorry, but. Hey. That's wrong. No, I never. I don't want
your job—Are you kidding? Well, fuck you. Just fuck you.
Fuck you! Christ! *(Hangs up.)*

JILL. *(Enters. She has been in the kitchen, and there is
baby food streaked in her hair.)* Who was that?

RYAN. I'm having an affair.

JILL. Give me the baby.

RYAN. I'm holding her. I'm having an affair.

JILL. *(Sits, heavily.)* All right.

RYAN. *(A long beat.)* Somebody I met at work.

JILL. I really should nurse her. My breasts are full.
Look. There's milk coming through my dress. *(Takes the
baby.)*

RYAN. I'm having an affair.

JILL. I heard you.

RYAN. Put the baby down. Put the baby down.

JILL. She's nursing.

RYAN. Put her down.

JILL. She'll cry.

RYAN. Put the baby down or I will walk out that door!

*(JILL takes the baby offstage.
Enter JILL.
During the following, the BABY's crying gets louder and
more frantic.
RYAN goes close to Jill.)*

RYAN. We lived together for seven years in the dead
center of a heat that kept blazing—

JILL. Can I go in to her?

RYAN. We used to know, we used to understand without the slightest semblance of a doubt that we together the two of us could be a wall against the ocean of banality, a fortress!

JILL. Can I go in to her?

RYAN. And now you're content to see me go every day to a place where people crucify each other over the number of lines on a piece of paper. Paper!

(*JILL starts to go toward the baby.*
RYAN turns her around, rips her dress down the front and sucks at her breast.
Beat.
JILL pushes him away, and goes in to the crying baby.)

RYAN. I am not worthless!

JILL. (*Re-enters with the suckling baby, sits in the rocking chair.*) I don't know. I suppose I should be hysterical. You're having an affair. I hear it's what a lot of men do. And now I guess I should tell you that you must never go in to work, to that woman, every again. (*Beat.*) Just stay in your job. Just a few more months. And I'll wean her. I'll start right away. And when she's no longer nursing, maybe I can find a job and you can stay home with her. And we'll be close again.

(*BLACKOUT.*
LIGHTS up again on the bedroom. The middle of the night.
RYAN and JILL sleep, backs turned toward each other. There is no movement or sound for a long beat.
LIGHTS up on the runway. Nobody is there.
The earth-shattering sound of an AIRPLANE coming, passing overhead.

*In his sleep RYAN is momentarily shaken by a tremor,
    but HE sleeps on.
BLACKOUT the bedroom and the runway.
LIGHTS up on the conference table.
SAUL is gone.
LILA is reading something.
BARRY watches tensely.
RYAN plays with a pencil.)*

    LILA. (*Puts down the paper.*) Good. And this?
    BARRY. The first run of the Cold Calls Form.
    LILA. (*Picks it up.*) Oh, yes. Then we're on schedule?
    BARRY. To the day, Lila. Ryan's been handling it.
    LILA. Good, Ryan. You're a dependable young man.

(*RYAN is silent.*)

    BARRY. Thank you.
    LILA. Is everything all right, Ryan? I can't help but
notice that you've been very—quiet—for quite some
time—ever since, perhaps, Saul—
    BARRY. He knows, we all know you did exactly what
had to be done—
    LILA. Please, Barry, for God's sake, let the boy speak!
Is everything all right?
    RYAN. Everything is fine, Lila. Thank you.
    LILA. The baby?
    RYAN. Fine.
    LILA. Are you losing sleep?
    RYAN. No, my—wife gets up with her. Mostly.
Nursing.
    LILA. Well, then, perhaps the time of year. I know I
used to get very depressed in the Fall. Not any more. One
of the great blessings of getting older is that one can
finally be free of all these demands of nature. (*To Ryan.*) I

hope you know that you can come to me and talk to me. I
hope you know that you can do that.

(*No response from Ryan.*)

LILA. Okay. Where were we? Yes. (*Examines the Cold
Calls Form.*) Good. Good. Wait a minute. Explain
something to me, Barry.
BARRY. Yes, what is it, Lila?
LILA. Here where it says Call Taken By.
BARRY. Yes.
LILA. There're only two lines.
BARRY. Yes?
LILA. But we agreed on three lines.
BARRY. (*Beat.*) Omigod. Thank goodness you noticed.
LILA. How many of these have we had printed?
BARRY. Sixty thousand.
LILA. At what cost?
BARRY. Under twelve thousand dollars.
LILA. What the hell is the meaning of this? Do I have
twelve thousand dollars to throw away? Don't we have an
approval process in this place? Haven't we been over this
and over this? Who sent this out? Am I hiring
nincompoops? Who is responsible for this?
BARRY. (*Beat.*) I am. It's my department. You're
right. I should've kept a closer tab on—
RYAN. No! I am! I authorized those two fucking lines
on that piece of paper! I did the accursed deed, and do you
know why, Lila, do you know why? Because you told me
to. Yes. You told me to!

(*JILL II appears in the conference room, naked or wearing
the transparent, mythic gown. During the following
RYAN stands and moves toward Jill II, but continues
speaking to Lila.*)

RYAN. (*To Lila.*) The very best thing would be for you to leave this place, and go where it's hot, and take off your clothing, and lie in the hot sand, and let the ocean rise between your legs.

(*BLACKOUT.*
LIGHTS up on a space.
RYAN and JILL are fighting.)

RYAN. Literalism makes the world of abstract materialism, of dead matter of the human body as dead matter. Literalism kills everything, including the human body ...

(*Overlapping:*)

JILL. Dishes! Forks! Spoons! Soap!
RYAN. It is the spirit Blake called Ulro, which sees nothing but rock and sand, jostling together in the void ...
JILL. Soap suds! Vitamins! Eye dropper! Mouth!
RYAN. Literalism makes a universe of stone, and men astonished, petrified. Literalism is the ministration of death, written and engraved in stones, tables of stone and stony heart ...

(*The ROAR of the crowd.*)

JILL. Telephone! Refrigerator! Magnets!
RYAN. The incarnation of symbols gives us a new heart, a heart for the first time human, a heart for the first time made of flesh ...
JILL. (*Becoming uncertain.*) Eye dropper ... Mouth ...

(*The BUZZER.*)

RYAN. (*Gaining strength.*) A new heart also will I give you, and and a new spirit will I put within you, and I will take away the stony heart out of your flesh ...

JILL. Teeth ... Breast ... Nipple ... Nipple ...

(*The BUZZER.*)

RYAN. Incarnation is the word made flesh. Refrain from uniting with words, in order to unite with the word made flesh!

(*The ROAR of the crowd grows. RYAN is winning.*)

JILL. (*Is searching for the word, find it.*) Milk!

(*The crowd is HUSHED, then ROARS its approval.*)

JILL. Milk! Milk! Milk! Milk! Milk! Milk!

RYAN. (*Speaking faster and faster, panicky.*) The abstractions idolized by literalism are words; words detached from the breath of living bodies; detached from the breath of life, the spirit, and hardened into independent reality ...

JILL. (*Gaining strength.*) Milk! Milk! Milk! Milk! Milk! Milk!

RYAN. (*Growing weak.*) ... words written down, scripture, the dead letter; Latin litera, the letter; Greek gamma, the writing. (*Grows weaker.*) The letter is alienated spirit, what Augustine calls the letter ... written outside ... the man ... (*Falls, defeated.*)

JILL. (*Laughing ecstatically, hands raised in a gesture of triumph.*) Milk!

(*BLACKOUT.*

LIGHTS up on the bedroom. Enter JILL. SHE is smoking a cigarette. SHE sits in the rocking chair.)

JILL. Ryan did leave his job. And he left me, too. He went back to Alaska. I got work editing. Free-lance. I do quite a lot for Price, in fact. Lila Price seems to feel somewhat—responsible for us. I hear from Ryan from time to time. Sends me money when he can, like a few hundred bucks for Katie's braces last spring. And once in awhile, he puts in a little note. Like this one. *(Takes a note from her pocket. Reads.)* Once in the absolute sheer terror of the first glimmering of the chasm that had come between us, which comes to my mind, today, Jill, because I have climbed today to the top of the glacier, and stood today at the very precipice of the fissure that runs miles deep through those blue walls, and looked into it, and thought of falling, I lied to you. I told you that I was having an affair. But I was never having an affair. I was only hopelessly in love, Jill, with the fire and the ice. *(Puts her cigarette to the note, and it flames up, burns, falls.)* What a luxury, Ryan. So indulge. I am still here, changed forever by the necessities of milk.

End of play

Note: The portion of the above speech which represents Ryan's note (Once ... ice) may be read by Jill or read by Ryan in a spotlight. The playwright leaves this to the discretion of the director.

The "death" portion of the evening.

The End of I

A one-act comedy

The End of I was first presented at the West Bank Cafe, New York, on January 24, 1989, with the following cast:

JEROME..James Gleason
CURTIS..Paul Mantell
ALICE.. Kathryn Rosseter

Director ....Anita Khanzadian

CHARACTERS

JEROME (late thirties)
CURTIS (late thirties)
ALICE (late thirties)

TIME: The Present
SETTING: Composite set representing a mountain-top, a bedroom, and a city street.

THE END OF I

Scene 1

Nighttime. A country road. A full MOON. CRICKETS.
Before the LIGHTS rise, JEROME and CURTIS shout,
*   overlapping:*

JEROME. Wee-haw! Start 'er up! Let's go! Open 'er
up!
    CURTIS. All right! Here we go! Away! Let 'er rip!
Charge!

(The LIGHTS rise on JEROME and CURTIS sitting on
*   their motorcycles. THEY are leaning forward in a*
*   posture of eager anticipation as if they're just about to*
*   take off.*
Overlapping:)

JEROME. Eeeh-hee! Here we go! Fuck, let's mix 'er up!
Go! Go! Go!
    CURTIS. Woo-hoo! Charge! Charge! Move! Go! Go!
Go go go go!

(NEITHER MAN moves.)

CURTIS. It's not working.
    JEROME. It will.
    CURTIS. I think we lost it, I think we really lost it.
    JEROME. If we lost it, we can find it.
    CURTIS. We've been sitting here for, God, almost an
hour, look, if I don't get home soon, Pammy'll kill me.
    JEROME. Pammy! Where does Pammy keep your balls
since she cut them off?

CURTIS. That's not like you.

(*JEROME takes out a flask.*)

CURTIS.What's that?
JEROME. Apple juice.
CURTIS. You're not going to start drinking now?
JEROME. Damn right I am.
CURTIS. You think I'm gonna ride with you plastered?
JEROME. You used to ride with me plastered, you used to ride with me blottoed, you used to ride with me upside down.
CURTIS. That was before—
JEROME. Don't mention it—
CURTIS. Before—
JEROME. Don't talk about it!
CURTIS. Put that thing away. If you don't put that thing away, Jerome Corsky, you won't be riding this hill tonight.
JEROME. Don't talk to me in your goddamn teacher voice, you're not in any goddamn classroom now. (*Puts away flask.*) Okay, damnit! Wee-haw! Shit!, let 'er ride! Ride! Ride!
CURTIS. Okay! Out we go! In we go! On we go! Over we go!

(*THEY don't move.*)

CURTIS. We lost it.

(*During the following, CURTIS lags behind Jerome, but catches up with increasing vigor.*)

JEROME.
I, Jerome Corsky, do
hereby pledge, to my bike
When I'm with you
I won't hurry
I won't worry

I won't think what could
be
I won't think what would
be
All I'm gonna do is
Ride
I won't judge
I won't fudge
I won't coddle no boss

I won't regret no loss
All I'm gonna do is
Ride
I won't look back
I won't detract
All I'm gonna do is
All I'm gonna do is
Ride
And when I ride,
I'm gonna ride high,
Touch the sky,
With my pals by my
side,
I'm gonna fly free
This road and me.

CURTIS.
Come on. I don't remember
it. That was when we had
twenty-five guys ... When I.
Curtis Spoonfellow.
Do hereby pledge to
my bike
When I'm with you
I won't hurry
I won't worry
I won't hurry
I won't worry
I won't think what would be
I won't think what could be
(*Correcting himself.*) would
be—

(*Catching up.*)
All I'm gonna do is
Ride
I won't judge I won't
fudge I won't coddle no boss
regret no loss
All I'm gonna do is
Ride
I won't look back
I won't detract
All I'm gonna do is
All I'm gonna do is
Ride
And when I ride,
I'm gonna ride high,
Touch the sky,
My pals by my side,
I'm gonna fly free

I, Jerome Corsky,	This road and me.
Do hereby pledge	I, Curtis Spoonfellow,
I'm gonna	Do hereby pledge
Ride!	I'm gonna Ride!

(*THEY end on a upbeat, obviously exhilarated.*)

JEROME. Goddamn that can still do it, I should've been a poet, Curtis, I should've been a goddamn poet.

CURTIS. You're a poet, Jerry, you really are. By the way, it's "this road and I" ...

JEROME. What?

CURTIS. In the pledge. If you want to be a poet, it's not correct to say "this road and *me*, " it's "this road and *I*."

JEROME. That doesn't rhyme.

CURTIS. Yeah, but it could, see, just take out the "free," just make a little change—

JEROME. I don't want to make a little change. Who the hell wants to make a little change?

CURTIS. The rules of good grammar—

JEROME. Fuck! ... the rules of good grammar. What has happened to you? What the hell has happened to you? What has happened to all of us? What the hell has happened to all of us?

CURTIS. You know what happened—

JEROME. Don't mention it—

CURTIS. You gotta want to talk about it—

(*Viciously, JEROME starts up his MOTORCYCLE. CURTIS takes the cue and starts his MOTORCYCLE. THEY sit there, revving their MOTORCYCLES. CURTIS turns off this MOTORCYCLE. After quite awhile, JEROME turns off his MOTORCYCLE.*)

CURTIS. We lost it.

JEROME. Must you keep saying that?

CURTIS. Look, why don't we just pack up, put the bikes back on the truck, go home, have a beer, maybe stop for a beer, okay? All the other guys dropped out long ago, even before—

JEROME. Don't mention it!

CURTIS. Even before Marty—

JEROME. Don't mention it, I tell you!

CURTIS. Don't you want to talk about it?

JEROME. Not here. Not now.

CURTIS. Okay, not here, not now, then let's make a date— (*Takes out his appointment book.*) What's good for you? I'm free two days this week after school, no, wait, Thursday I have to take Glinda to the dentist, Friday might be good if we can do it close, wait, or at least halfway between—

(*JEROME jumps off his bike, and grabs Curtis' appointment book.*)

CURTIS. Hey!

JEROME. You bring your appointment book with you on the bike?

CURTIS. You bring your whiskey.

JEROME. Whiskey belongs with motorcycles, appointment books belong with goddamn briefcases!

CURTIS. That's in the truck. Look, I thought I might have time on the way home, I'd check my lesson plans, if you're driving, what's wrong with that—

JEROME. We're here on the mountain! You forgot what it means to be here on the mountain on our bikes?

(*THEY are both silent for a moment. The sound of the CRICKETS is very loud. JEROME returns Curtis's book.*)

JEROME. Curt. If we don't ride soon, you know we're never gonna ride again. Tick tick tick one by one you do everything for the last time. You ride for the last time. You make love for the last time. You breathe for the last time. And you don't even know it. Are you ready to say you've ridden for the last time?

CURTIS. Well, I'd sure rather ride for the last time than breathe for the last time.

JEROME. (*Overlapping.*) You're missing my whole point.

CURTIS. I think I got your whole point.

JEROME. My point is that you've got to guard against this creeping last–timism, you can't let it get you—

CURTIS. You're talking about Marty, that's who you're talking about, you're talking about Marty, Marty—

JEROME. (*Shouts.*) I am not talking about Marty! Damn you! Curt. I'm sorry. I know I've been an unbelievable shit lately—

CURTIS. You really have—

JEROME. Because I haven't been getting any sleep, I've been so worried about—about everything, but I'm not ready to say I'm never going to ride again. Are you?

CURTIS. I don't know. Maybe I am. Why should we of everybody, of the whole gang, be the last ones out here? I mean I could make, next year I could make assistant principal, when the Russian delegation came to my school, they came to *my* classroom. Mine. TV camera and all. I learned how to say "zdrastvuge." Hello. What would the the Russian delegation think if they knew I was up here riding tonight?

JEROME. What the hell do you care what the Russian delegation thinks?

CURTIS. It's just that you can't help noticing the enormous disparity, the gulf, even, between what the

Russian delegation thinks of me and me here on this bike—

JEROME. Fuck! I'll tell you what the Russian delegation would think, I'll tell you what the Russian delegation would think, they'd think, look at that bitchin' machine, jeezus, I wish I had me a machine like that baby, that's what they'd think.

CURTIS. They would never use the work "bitchin'."

JEROME. For Chrissake—

CURTIS. I met them!

JEROME. Curtis. Don't fail me. Don't fail me, buddy. You and me—

CURTIS. I.

JEROME. You and I were riding before the rest of 'em. Remember the thrill. Taking a curve like it was inside your own spine, you forget to think, you just move, time stops but you're still moving like a goddamn tiger pure reflex. It's so good. Please. Let's give it one more chance. Please. Tomorrow night, same place same time.

CURTIS. Tomorrow night? (*Checks appointment book.*) Maybe tomorrow night, no, not tomorrow night, I promised Pammy I'd help her with the pastry crust for the big dinner party, I have it right here, (*Shows book.*), "crust"—

JEROME. Please!

CURTIS. Her manager will be there. Not that she has a manager, she doesn't really have a manager, I mean she *has* a manager, but the manager couldn't manage without Pammy ...

JEROME. Please! Buddy!

CURTIS. Okay, buddy. (*Takes a fancy fountain pen set from his leather jacket pocket, makes an insertion in his appointment book.*) Wednesday October twelve. Ride with Jerry on Crystal Mountain. Could we make it nine-fifteen? (*LIGHTS down.*)

Scene 2

LIGHTS up. Later than night. Jerome and Alice's bedroom.

At first glance, THEY are both asleep. However, it soon becomes apparent that JEROME is not asleep at all: HE is suffering an acute attack of insomnia. HE thrashes; turns over and over; turns the pillow over and over; punches the pillow; tries his head on all corners of the pillow; tries his feet on the pillow; adjusts the covers; sticks his feet out; puts his feet in; maniacally turns on a mini-light and reads; pretends to get drowsy; pretends to snore; puts his head at the foot of the bed; puts his head on Alice's stomach; throws his entire body across Alice; hangs his head off the bed, etc. etc. HE is in torment.

JEROME. Alice.
ALICE. Mm.
JEROME. I can't sleep.
ALICE. Go to sleep.
JEROME. I can't sleep again.
ALICE. Mm.
JEROME. I can't sleep again, Alice. Alice.
ALICE. Shh.
JEROME. I'm sorry to wake you.
ALICE. Shh.
JEROME. I'm sorry to wake you.
ALICE. It's okay.
JEROME. I can't sleep.
ALICE. Sleep.
JEROME. I can't sleep.

ALICE. Sleep.
JEROME. Alice.
ALICE. Mm.
JEROME. What is death?
ALICE. We'll figure it out in the morning.
JEROME. You always say that. You always say we'll figure it out in the morning, but how will we figure it out? Do you know how to figure it out? I've been trying for three weeks to figure it out, and I can't figure anything out. I can't figure a damn thing out. Did it ever occur to you that death could be nothing? Nothing, Alice. Nothing. Nothing. Nothing. Death could be nothing. Nothing, Alice. Death could be absolutely nothing. Can you figure out nothing? Can you? Can you figure out nothing? Can you find nothing? Can you experience nothing? Can you *be* nothing? Try to *be* nothing. Go ahead, Alice. I dare you. Try it. (*ALICE is asleep.*) Try it. Try to be nothing. Try it. Just try it, Alice. Just try it. Just try it for one minute. For one second. Try it. Just try to *be* nothing. Not just nothing, nothingness. Try to be nothingness for one minute. For one second. Absolutely nothing. I don't mean something. I don't mean wake-up-in-a-few-hours. I mean nothing. Nothing. No thing, nothing. No feel. No smell. No taste. No see. No nothing. No nothing. No me. No I. No I. (*HE bolts upright, extremely agitated.*) Alice. Alice. (*HE shakes HER awake.*)
ALICE. Come here, darling.
JEROME. No! Don't tempt me! You fall into a woman's arms you can't even begin to understand nothing, nothing just disappears, nothing just evaporates, all around you there's something, something, something. Women are very dangerous, Alice. (*ALICE is asleep.*) Women make you believe that you're going to live forever. And you're not going to live forever. You're going to die! Die! Die! Die! Die! Stay away from me, Alice! Alice. Alice! Oh

God, I love you, I love you, Alice, I love you. I love you, I love you. I love you. I love you and I love our daughters. I love their eyes, I love their hair, I love their little fingernails. I love their tiny shoes. I love those little sheets you bought them, the ones with the butterflies. (*Notices the sheet under him.*) I love this sheet. I love this sheet! (*Rubs the sheet.*) I don't want to leave this sheet! I don't want to! I love it! I love this sheet! I don't want to! Would it go on without me? Could it go on without me? Could it? Would it? Where would I be? Where's Marty, Alice? What happened to Marty? Where did he go? One minute he was riding his motorcycle, zooming with the wind on his face more alive that at any other time except inside a woman and the next minute, blotto! Gone! Zap! Disappeared! *People disappear off this planet, Alice. All the time.* Can't you save me? Can't your love save me? Save me, Alice, save me!

ALICE. In the morning.

JEROME. (*Speaks directly into her face.*) You and me are going to die, Alice.

ALICE. Come here, sweetheart. (*Opens her arms to him.*)

JEROME. No! No!

(*ALICE makes murmuring, comforting sounds. JEROME succumbs and collapses into her arms. SHE continues to comfort him like a baby.*)

ALICE. There. Better?

JEROME. Oh, yes, oh God, yes.

ALICE. Everything is all right.

JEROME. We're not going to die?

ALICE. Probably not tonight.

JEROME. But I could die tomorrow, Alice. I'm going out on my motorcycle.

ALICE. Drive carefully, dear.

JEROME. Marty drove carefully and he strangely disappeared. (*ALICE is dozing off.*) Do you love me, Alice? (*ALICE snores.*) Do you love me? Alice? (*ALICE makes comforting sound. Urgently.*) Do you love me?

ALICE. (*Shakes herself awake.*) Of course I do.

JEROME. Say it.

ALICE. I love you.

JEROME. Say it with my name.

ALICE. I love you, Jerry.

JEROME. You don't love me. (*SHE starts to object.*) Would you let me take this sheet with me on my motorcycle?

ALICE. This sheet? Certainly not. This is one of my best sheets.

JEROME. You love this sheet more than you love me.

ALICE. What are you talking about?

JEROME. Why do you let me go out on my motorcycle?

ALICE. Let you?

JEROME. All the other wives stopped their husbands long ago, even before Marty died. All the other wives made terrific stinks about their husbands going out on motorcycles.

ALICE. You think they're bitches.

JEROME. Maybe I'd rather live with a bitch than die with a saint!

ALICE. (*Carefully.*) You've been riding your bike for twenty years. Since long before I met you. Of course, at times I wish you'd stop. Lately. But I haven't felt I had the right to ask that of you. I know what that motorcycle means to you. Sometimes I think you'd die without it.

(*Beat. Overlapping.*)

JEROME. Thank you, thank you, you're the most wonderful woman any man ever had, I swear you're a goddamn—

ALICE. If you want me to be more pushy, I'll be more pushy—

JEROME. Angel—No, no, I don't want you to be more pushy—

ALICE. If you want me to be more pushy, just tell me and I can be more pushy—

JEROME. Don't be more pushy, I don't want you to be more pushy—

ALICE. Tell me and I'll be much more pushy, much more pushy—

JEROME. (*Shouts.*) No, goddammit, don't be more pushy!

ALICE. You know, you're very angry.

JEROME. I'm not angry.

ALICE. You're angry at the whole world. You've been angry at the whole world since Marty died, it breaks my heart that you had to be there when your friend died, honey, but at some point you have to start getting over it. Try to take your mind off it. Do something you enjoy. Go in the garage and fix a hubcap. Or how 'bout a nice snack? Turkey sandwich? Chocolate cookies? I have chocolate cookies with double chips, double fudge chips! Or we could just—stay—here—we could just—lie down—put you to sleep—

JEROME. No! I can't. I can't right now. I'm sorry I can't.

ALICE. We could try.

JEROME. I can't!

ALICE. (*Sexily.*) I could be more pushy.

JEROME. No. Don't be more pushy.

(*LIGHTS down.*)

Scene 3

LIGHTS up on the country road, the next evening.
JEROME and CURTIS are sitting on their motorcycles.
THEIR eyes are closed. THEY remain this way for
several beats before speaking.

JEROME. You have something?

CURTIS. (*Resentfully.*) Maybe.

JEROME. Okay, you start.

CURTIS. Why should I start? This was your idea.

JEROME. You said you have something. I don't have
anything.

CURTIS. You're supposed to be the big poet.

JEROME. I'm an accountant.

CURTIS. Yeah, but you're *supposed* to be the big poet.
So start.

JEROME. Okay. Brave.

CURTIS. (*Reluctantly.*) Strong.

JEROME. Immortal.

CURTIS. Free.

JEROME. Wild.

CURTIS. Complete.

JEROME. Transformed.

CURTIS. Whole. No, wait. Whole is the same as
complete.

JEROME. No, it isn't, it's okay.

CURTIS. No, no, it's the same thing, really. I'll think
of something else.

JEROME. It's not the same thing. Whole. Fine.
Whole. —

CURTIS. I don't want to use "whole."

JEROME. You can use "whole."

CURTIS. I can't, really, not if I use "complete," one or the other. Which should I throw out?

JEROME. You can use them both, goddammit.

CURTIS. They mean exactly the same thing.

JEROME. They don't, no, they don't, and even if they do, who the fuck cares, let's get on—

CURTIS. On the other hand, maybe they don't mean exactly the same thing. There is a subtle difference, perhaps, think about it, "whole" can apply to something that is of one piece, can't it, whereas "complete" may but does not necessarily imply that which is potentially composed of many different parts.

JEROME. (*Sarcastically.*) Oh, for Chrissake, why don't you get out your dictionary, why don't you consult your goddamn dictionary—

CURTIS. All right. (*Takes a dictionary from his leather jacket, opens eyes.*)

JEROME. (*Opens his eyes.*) You have a dictionary? Why do you need a dictionary at the top of the mountain?

CURTIS. For situations just such as this.

JEROME. Put that thing away. Get that goddamn thing out of my—(*Threateningly, dismounts.*)

CURTIS. If you come anywhere near me I'll take my dictionary and my motorcycle and put them in the truck and drive back to the city and leave you here alone. I'll do it!

JEROME. I'm sorry.

CURTIS. (*Puts away dictionary.*) Now let's get on with your stupid game. Although it's not going to help. We've lost it.

(*THEY close their eyes.*)

JEROME. Happy.
CURTIS. Free.

JEROME. Happy.
CURTIS. You said that already.
JEROME. You can say things twice.
CURTIS. Free.
JEROME. Happy.
CURTIS. Free.

(*A peaceful energy starts to overtake them as THEY say these two words over and over.*)

JEROME. Happy.
CURTIS. Free.
JEROME. Happy.
CURTIS. Free.
JEROME. Happy.
CURTIS. Free.
JEROME. Happy.
CURTIS. Free.
JEROME. Yes. That's how we used to feel when we rode our bikes.
CURTIS. Happy.
JEROME. Free. And safe.
CURTIS. Safe.
JEROME. Yes. We felt safe. Were we blind?
CURTIS. We didn't believe we could die, in those days.
JEROME. We didn't believe it. But now we know we can die.
CURTIS. Yes. We know we can.
JEROME. We know we will.
CURTIS. Some day.
JEROME. Any day. I don't want to.
CURTIS. Nobody wants to.
JEROME. I don't want to! If I could only believe that there were a paradise after death where I'd go and ride my bike and write poems ... People believe things like that.

The Mormons believe that everyone in heaven owns a two-bedroom ranch house. The Hindus believe that you go around chanting and bathing in white light. Why can't I believe that?

CURTIS. That's not what the Hindus believe. The Hindus believe in various levels of post-death experience, which actually correspond to the seven chakras of the spinal—

JEROME. Shut up. Shut up! Shut up!! You know what your problem is? You know? Your problem is that you're afraid to look at the big picture, all you see is details—

(*Overlapping, their eyes still closed:*)

CURTIS. Oh, yeah, is that my problem?
JEROME. Little, teeny, insignificant details—
CURTIS. Is that my problem?
JEROME. Details that couldn't interest a snail.
CURTIS. (*Cuts through, opens eyes.*) Who's the one who's afraid to talk about Marty? Hah? Is that me? Or you?
JEROME. (*Opens eyes.*) I'm not afraid to talk about Marty.
CURTIS. Bullshit you aren't.
JEROME. I'm not afraid to talk about Marty. I talk about Marty all the time at home, with Alice. Only I don't want to talk about Marty here. Here and now we're supposed to be doing one thing and that's ride! Ride! That's all we're supposed to be doing! Is just ride! Ride!
CURTIS. But we can't ride, because ... (*Overcome with curiosity.*) He died on this hill ... You were with him ... Going around the same curve ... What did he look like? After—?
JEROME. An arm was lying next to a rock. The hand was open and the fingers were twitching.

CURTIS. Oh.

JEROME. Happy. (*Beat.*) Happy. (*Beat.*) **Happy.** (*Beat.*)

CURTIS. Let's pack it up, Jerry.

JEROME. No.

CURTIS. My thighs are killing me.

JEROME. Your thighs?

CURTIS. Look, I'm not as limber as I used to be.

JEROME. You're thinking about your goddamn thighs?

CURTIS. They're killing me.

JEROME. (*Sarcastically.*) Why didn't you bring your heating pad?

CURTIS. I did, it's in the truck, well, it's not exactly a heating pad, it's a kind of portable Vap-O-Rub applicator—

JEROME. Vap-O-Rub! We're fighting for our lives and you're thinking about Vap-O-Rub!

(*Overlapping:*)

CURTIS. Tough guy—

JEROME. You have no idea what this means, do you? You don't know what's at stake!

CURTIS. Back off, tough guy—

JEROME. His appointment book, his fountain pen, his lesson plans, his dictionary, his heating pad, his goddamn life is at stake!

CURTIS. After all the trouble you caused me!

JEROME. His goddamn life—

CURTIS. Trouble!

JEROME. What trouble did I fuckin' cause you, trouble, tonight or any other night? ... Huh?

CURTIS. Don't you see this? (*Shows a bruise on the side of his head.*) You're so wrapped up in yourself you don't even notice anyone else.

JEROME. What's that?

CURTIS. Pammy threw a wooden spoon at me, not really wooden, woodgrain, missed my eye by an inch, I still haven't gotten all the pastry batter out of my ear.

JEROME. What came over her?

CURTIS. She doesn't want me to ride anymore. She screams like a banshee every time she sees me walk out with my helmet.

JEROME. (*Beat. Starts to laugh.*) You know, you wouldn't know your dick it if came up and shook your hand.

CURTIS. What?

JEROME. If your dick put on a grass skirt and did the hula, you wouldn't recognize it.

CURTIS. What are you saying?

JEROME. If you got served your dick on a hot dog roll, you'd add mustard and relish. And it would be Pammy (*Laughing.*), it would be Pammy—Pammy—who served it to you.

(*CURTIS reaches around and slugs JEROME, who pulls back and then slumps forward on his motorcycle.*)

JEROME. I don't know what's happening to me.

CURTIS. I used to really look up to you.

JEROME. I'm turning into a first-class asshole.

CURTIS. I'm going home. (*Dismounts, begins to lead bike offstage, stops.*)

(*JEROME kick-starts his MOTORCYCLE and revs it.*)

CURTIS. (*Turns around.*) Turn that thing off and stop acting like an idiot. Turn if off, Jerry! Turn it off!

JEROME. (*Spills out.*) I'm terrified, Curt, I'm terrified, I got death in my bones, I'm infected with death, I sleep, eat and dream death, if I don't ride my bike tonight I'm going to die, I know I'm going to die. (*Sobs.*)

CURTIS. (*Comes toward him.*) Jerry— (*Turns his bike around and walks it parallel to Jerome's, mounts and KICK-STARTS it.*)

JEROME. (*Overlapping, weakly:*) Let's go! Here we go! Wee-ha! Ride!

CURTIS. Okay! Open 'er up! Into the night! Onto the road!

(*THEY don't move. After awhile, CURTIS turns off his MOTORCYCLE, dismounts and turns off Jerome's MOTORCYCLE. CURTIS and JEROME embrace.*)

JEROME. Let's try one more time.

CURTIS. For Chrissake.

JEROME. One more time! We don't have to come up here to this hill, we'll just ride around Brooklyn. On Saturday. In the afternoon. What can happen in goddamn Brooklyn on Saturday in the afternoon? We'll go thirty miles an hour, we'll wear our helmets, we'll stop at every stop sign and wave at every cop, we'll pass on the left, I just want to feel this thing vibrating between my legs one last time—Please!

CURTIS. (*Beat.*) All right! But I can't tell Pammy. (*Checks appointment book.*) She does aerobics Saturday in the morning, no, she changed to the afternoon, she didn't like the morning instructor, she said he did steps Baryshnikov couldn't follow and she's some dancer, too, she'll be out from, say, three to four-thirty, we'd have to make it quick—very quick—just an hour to ride.

JEROME. That's all I want. Just an hour to ride.

(*LIGHTS down.*)

Scene 4

LIGHTS up. Later that night.
Jerome and Alice's bedroom. ALICE is asleep in the bed.
JEROME sits in an easy chair. HE is dishevelled and
unshaven. Suddenly, JEROME howls. ALICE bolts up
in bed. During the following, JEROME continues to
howl.

ALICE. What—? Are you still over there? You come to bed this minute. This minute, Jerry. Come to bed this minute. This minute! Jerry. Jerry, honey. Oh God, you'll wake the girls. Stop it now, Jerry. Stop it. Stop it. I'm going to call the police. I'm going to call the doctor.

JEROME. Nobody can help.

ALICE. Thank God. You're talking.

JEROME. After death there is nothing, Alice. Nothing.

ALICE. I don't think so, sweetheart. I don't see how that could be. And even if it is, honey, there's worse things ... Imagine living inside of fire forever, the nuns used to say you burn and burn perpetually, you can smell your own skin toasting and watch your body melting forever—

JEROME. (*Frantically, prayerfully.*) Yes, yes! I want to! I want to!

ALICE. You need help, Jerry.

JEROME. But there isn't any.

ALICE. You need help.

JEROME. But don't you see there isn't any! Can't you get that through your thick skull?

ALICE. I can't go on like this. The girls can't go on like this. Today you were too tired to go to work. And you haven't touched me—

JEROME. Bring that up—

ALICE. Haven't touched me—

JEROME. Just like a woman—

ALICE. You haven't said one kind word to me in weeks!

JEROME. (*Viciously.*) Just like a woman to carry on about touching and kind words!

ALICE. (*Beat.*) We've got to get you some kind of help.

JEROME. Help? Help? (*Jumps up, paces.*) Help? Don't you see? The entire history of the human race is an endeavor to find some kind of help. Entire religions have been founded trying to find some kind of help. Whole nations have marched to war trying to find some kind of help. Cathedrals have been built. Libraries have been filled. Billions of hapless individuals have spent billions and billions of hours engaged in millions and millions of nonsensical rituals all in the vain hope of finding some kind of help. So they wouldn't have to face the truth in their last moment on earth. That there's nothing after death, Alice. Nothing, nothing, nothing, nothing!

(*ALICE begins to unbutton her pajama top, looking at him hopefully, seductively.*)

JEROME. What are you doing? Don't do that. Button that. Button that. Button that.

(*JEROME throws a blanket around Alice so she is all wrapped up. Standing in the middle of the room, mummy-like, SHE begins to cry.*)

JEROME. Alice? Alice? Are you crying? Why are you crying, honey?

(*SHE cries louder.*)

JEROME. Alice? Don't cry. You don't like this blanket around you? Here, I'll take it off. (*Does so.*) I love your chest. I love your breasts, I love your throat. I love these buttons. But I can't. I can't, I can't.

ALICE. (*Takes the blanket off the floor.*) I'm going in to sleep with the girls.

JEROME. (*Stopping her.*) No, no, please don't do that. Don't do that. Don't leave me alone in here. The walls are soaked with death. Don't you feel it? Stay with me.

(*ALICE returns, gets into bed, and opens the blanket for Jerome. HE climbs into bed and puts his head on her shoulder. Several beats of silence.*)

JEROME. I haven't been much of a husband these past three weeks, have I? Since Marty died?

ALICE. No.

JEROME. We should try to do more things together, more things together, just the two of us, shouldn't we?

ALICE. (*Brightening.*) Yes! Yes, let's try to do more things together, just the two of us, all right!

JEROME. What would you like to do together—?

ALICE. Oh, I don't know, anything.

JEROME. It would be nice to do more things together.

ALICE. Oh, darling. What would you like to do together?

JEROME. Visualize death.

(*ALICE jumps away from him.*)

JEROME. That would be really good. That would be a really good thing for a husband and wife to do together. After all, we're going to be together, aren't we? On our deathbeds? Shouldn't we know what the other one is going through? Although it's not easy, visualizing death, believe me, I think with the two of us trying together, we could catch each other's little slip-ups, you know, like smelling, feeling, hearing the kids, maybe we could achieve that ultimate moment, that horrible, ultimate moment, the end of I—

ALICE. You've gone crazy, Jerry, you've gone crazy. The only thing you do normal anymore is riding your bike with Curtis and that's the most dangerous thing of all!

(*Beat. The following is very intense, as JEROME approaches her and SHE takes steps back.*)

JEROME. I do. I go out on my motorcycle with Curtis— (*Beat.*) But I leave Curtis far behind. I race like a madman past the black trees— (*Beat.*) And I race down the same hill where Marty died, I hold my breath round that same beautiful, deadly curve— (*Beat.*) And when I come out of it, I laugh! I laugh at the heavens and I laugh in Death's face, I defy Death to come anywhere near me. (*Laughs.*)

ALICE. (*Strong.*) Jerry! You are finished with your motorcycle! If I ever see you on your motorcycle ever again, ever see you anywhere near your motorcycle ever again, I will take the girls and pack up and go back to Washington! I don't care what you want! I love you! And I don't want you dead!

(*LIGHTS down.*)

Scene 5

LIGHTS up. The following Saturday afternoon.
A city street. ALICE and JEROME stand at the curb, arms
around each other, looking like young lovebirds. THEY
are silently sipping milkshakes through a straw.
CURTIS walks up, walking his MOTORCYCLE.

CURTIS. Hey, Alice!

ALICE. Curt.

CURTIS. Hey, buddy!

JEROME. (*HE has forgotten their date.*) Curt!—Hey, buddy. (*Gives him a high five.*)

CURTIS. Well I got the goddamn thing here, huh? I'll tell you, a bike, you know a bike is like, well it's one helluva thing when you got it between your legs but when you're walkin it's like an old lady it's just a pile of shit draggin metal, but, look, we got us some day, huh? To ride? Not a cloud in the sky. Actually I did see one cloud, off to the northeast as I was crossin De Graw ... But I'm ready. I'm ready! Where's your bike? Get your bike, let's go!

JEROME. I don't ride anymore.

CURTIS. What? Come on, let's go—

JEROME. I don't ride anymore—

CURTIS. You been bugging me all week, where's your motorcycle?

ALICE. He sold it.

CURTIS. Sold—? He would never sell his motorcycle, he loves his motorcycle.

ALICE. Yesterday, to a Columbia student.

CURTIS. Did he get a good price? Forget it, what the hell, you're getting a new bike, right?

JEROME. No, Curt. I'm not riding anymore.

CURTIS. Not riding—? Come on.

JEROME. I've lost it, buddy.

CURTIS. Hey. C'mon. That's up at the mountain, sure, we gotta start slow, hey, c'mon, what can happen on a Brooklyn street, huh, we'll pass on the left, stop at every stop sign, hey, I only have (*Checks watch.*) thirty-seven more minutes then I gotta get home, Pammy's not only expecting me she's expecting me to have the turkey in the oven, with stuffing, I gotta chop the almonds, hey, you're kidding, right? Right? One more little joke just to set me up, I know, your bike's right around the corner, right? And maybe you even got six of the ol' gang together to surprise me, right? And those machines are smokin. Right?

JEROME. There are no more machines, Curt. Only yours.

CURTIS. Okay. C'mon. Here. Try mine. Take it around the block. (*Begins to push his bike toward Jerome.*)

ALICE. No! Thanks very much, Curt, but don't bother. Jerry's riding days are over.

CURTIS. (*Suddenly, with viciousness.*) You made him do this.

ALICE. No! I wouldn't say that I made him, I—

CURTIS. You made him give up this thing I know, you know, he loves, he needs—

ALICE. I asked him if he would please stop because it was starting to affect the whole family—

CURTIS. You told him to—

ALICE. Okay! Yes! I told him to! I told him because he was begging me! He was begging me every day and every night to stop this crazy flinging himself in the face of death, for God's sake, you can't be boys forever!

CURTIS. (*Dismounts.*) Get on the bike, buddy.

(*Beat.*)

JEROME. (*Simply.*) ... No. I don't want to. I've lost it, buddy. I've lost the desire for it.

CURTIS. Could I have a sip of your milkshake?

JEROME. Sure.

CURTIS. What is it?

JEROME. Chocolate.

CURTIS. You've lost the desire?

JEROME. Yes.

CURTIS. This isn't real chocolate. The FDA has four thousand, two hundred and sixty-nine approved food colorings. They probably they probably they probably mixed seven, eight of them in there trying to make this look like real chocolate. I don't know if I can ride without you.

JEROME. You can ride without me. (*Takes the milkshake from Curtis's hand.*) Get on the bike—

CURTIS. I'll just walk it home. (*Begins to walk the bike upstage. Then HE gets on it, sits for a minute, turns the ignition key, rises, and comes down hard on the starter. There is the enormous explosion of the MOTORCYCLE starting. With enormous gusto–*) Wee-haw!

(*...And the LIGHTS fade.*)

End of Play

COSTUME PLOT

Scene 1 — Jerome and Curtis wear jeans and leather jackets

Scene 2 — Jerome and Alice wear pajamas

Scene 3 — Jerome and Curtis wear jeans and leather jackets

Scene 4 — Jerome and Alice wear pajamas. Alice's pajamas must button down the front.

Scene 5 — Jerome wears blue jean outfit without leather jacket. Curtis wears jeans and leather jacket. Alice is dressed casually.

PROPERTY PLOT

Furniture and furnishings

Two 36" stools
Chair
Bed with bedclothes
Two 18" stools
Counter
Mini-lamp or lamp

Other Props

Hip flask for whisky brought on by Jerome, Scene 1
Appointment book brought on by Curtis, Scene 1
Fountain pen set, brought on by Curtis, Scene 1
Pocket dictionary brought on by Curtis, Scene 3
Two milkshake containers with straws, brought on by
    Jerome and Alice, Scene 5

Flat (optional)

Stools representing motorcycles

Entrances

Chair

Bed

THE END OF I

— 14' —

— 13' —

Counter (scene 5)

stools

Flat (optional)

Notes: Bed should be raked o-
on a platform for sight lines.

Stools can represent motorcycles.

Other Publications for Your Interest

THE SQUARE ROOT OF LOVE
(ALL GROUPS—FOUR COMEDIES)

By DANIEL MELTZER

1 man, 1 woman—4 Simple Interiors

This full-length evening portrays four preludes to love—from youth to old age, from inno-cence to maturity. Best when played by a single actor and actress. **The Square Root of Love.** Two genius-level college students discover that Man (or Woman) does not live by intellectual pursuits alone . . . **A Good Time for a Change.** Our couple are now a suc-cessful executive and her handsome young male secretary. He has decided it's time for a change, and so has she . . . **The Battling Brinkmires.** George and Marsha Brinkmire, a middle-aged couple, have come to Haiti to get a ''quickie'' divorce. This one has a surprise ending . . . **Waiting For To Go.** We are on a jet waiting to take off for Florida. He's a re-tired plumbing contractor who thinks his life is over—she's a recent widow returning to her home in Hallandale. The play, and the evening, ends with a beginning . . . A success at off-off Broadway's Hunter Playwrights. Requires only minimal settings.   (#21314)

SNOW LEOPARDS
(LITTLE THEATRE—COMIC DRAMA)

By MARTIN JONES

2 women—Exterior

This haunting little gem of a play was a recent crowd-pleaser Off Off Broadway in New York City, produced by the fine StageArts Theatre Co. Set in Lincoln Park Zoo in Chicago in front of the snow leopards' pen, the play tells the story of two sisters from rural West Virginia. When we first meet Sally, she has run away from home to find her big sister Claire June, whose life Up North she has imagined to be filled with all the promise and hopes so lacking Down Home. Turns out, life in the Big City ain't all Sally and C.J. thought it would be: but Sally is going to stay anyway, and try to make her way. ''Affecting and carefully crafted . . . a moving piece of work.''—New York City Tribune. *Actresses take note*: this play is a treasure trove of scene and monologue material. *Producers take note*: the play may be staged simply and inexpensively.   (#21245)

Other Publications for Your Interest

ADVICE TO THE PLAYERS
(DRAMA)

By BRUCE BONAFEDE

5 men, 1 woman (interracial)—Interior

Seldom has a one-act play created such a sensation as did *Advice to the Players* at Actors Theatre of Louisville's famed Humana Festival of New American Plays. Mr. Bonafede has crafted an ingenious play about two Black South African actors, here in America to perform their internationally-acclaimed production of *Waiting for Godot*. The victims of persecution in their own country, here in the U.S. they become the victims of a different kind of persecution. The anti-apartheid movement wants a strong political gesture—they want the performance cancelled. And, they are willing to go to any lengths to achieve this aim—including threatening the families of the actors back home. Cleverly, Mr. Bonafede juxtaposes the predicament of Didi and Gogo in *Waiting for Godot* with the predicament of the two actors. Both, in an odd, ironic way, are Theatre of the Absurd. "A short play blazing with emotional force and moral complexities . . . taut, searing inquiry into the inequities frequently perpetrated in the name of political justice . . . a stunning moment of theatrical truth."—Louisville Courier-Journal.   (#3027)

APPROACHING LAVENDAR
(COMIC DRAMA)

By JULIE BECKETT CRUTCHER

3 women—Interior

While their father is marrying his fourth wife sardonic, controlled Jenny and her slightly neurotic housewife-sister Abigail wait in a church vestibule. There they encounter Wren, the spacey ingenue who is about to become their step-sister. The mood of polite tolerance degenerates with comic results as inherent tensions mount and the womens' conflicted feelings about their parents' remarriage surface. The contingent self-discovery results in new understanding and forgiveness, and ultimately reveals the significance of sisterhood. Highly-praised in its debut at the famed Actors Theatre of Louisville, the play was singled out by the Louisville press for its "precise and disquieting vision" as well as its sharp humor, as it "held a capacity audience rapt."   (#3649)

A TANTALIZING
(DRAMA)

By WILLIAM MASTROSIMONE

1 man, 1 woman—Interior

Originally produced by the amazing Actors Theatre of Louisville, this is a new one-act drama by the author of *The Woolgatherer* and *Extremities*. *A Tantalizing* is about the attempts by a young woman to "save" a street bum, a tattered and crazy old man whom she has dragged in off the street. Like Rose in *Extremities* she, too, has secrets in her closet. What these secrets are is the intriguing mystery in the plot of the play, as we gradually realize why the woman has taken such an interest in the bum.   (#22021)

Other Publications for Your Interest

PASTORAL
(COMEDY)

By PETER MALONEY

1 man, 1 woman—Exterior

Daniel Stern ("Blue Thunder", "Breaking Away") and Kristin Griffith ("The Europeans", "Interiors") starred originally at NYC's famed Ensemble Studio Theatre in the preceptive comedy about a city couple temporarily tending a farm. He hates the bucolic life and is terrified, for instance, by such horrors as a crowing rooster; whereas she is at one with the land *and* the rooster. "An endearing picture of young love at a comic crossroads."—N.Y. Times. "Sharp, satiric humor."—New Yorker. "An audience pleaser."—Village Voice. Published with *Last Chance Texaco*.   (#17995)

LAST CHANCE TEXACO
(DRAMA)

By PETER MALONEY

3 women—Interior

Originally staged to great acclaim at NYC's famed Ensemble Studio Theatre, this is a haunting, lyrical play set in the American Garage, a Texaco station in a small Texas town run by a mother and her daughter. Late one night, while driving through, a city woman named Ruth has a flat tire, an occurrence which causes her own unusual life to intersect with Verna and Cissy, as they fix her tire in the American Garage. This play is an excellent source of monologue and scene material. It is also a gripping piece of theatre. Published with *Pastoral*.   (#13887)

BUSINESSMAN'S LUNCH
(COMEDY)

By MICHAEL QUINN

4 men, 1 woman—Interior

Originally produced by the famed Actors Theatre of Louisville, this marked the debut of a wonderful new comic playwriting voice. We are in one of those quiche-and-salad restaurants, where three high-powered young executives of a nearby candy company are having lunch as they discuss company politics and various marketing and advertising strategies. They particularly enjoy making fun of one of their fellows who is not present, whom they consider a hopeless nerd—until, that is, they learn that he is engaged to marry the boss's daughter. "Cleverly skewers corporate stereotypes."—NY Times.   (#4712)